CAMBRIDGE | Discovery

KV-370-645

UNLOCK

READING & WRITING SKILLS

1

Andrew Scott

CALDERDALE
COLLEGE HALIFAX
LIBRARY RESOURCES

CAMBRIDGE
UNIVERSITY PRESS

CAMBRIDGE
UNIVERSITY PRESS

University Printing House, Cambridge CB2 8BS, United Kingdom

Cambridge University Press is part of the University of Cambridge.

It furthers the University's mission by disseminating knowledge in the pursuit of education, learning and research at the highest international levels of excellence.

www.cambridge.org
Information on this title: www.cambridge.org/9781107614017

© Cambridge University Press 2014

Content and images which are © Discovery Communications, LLC are reproduced here under license.

This publication is in copyright. Subject to statutory exception and to the provisions of relevant collective licensing agreements, no reproduction of any part may take place without the written permission of Cambridge University Press.

First published 2014

Printed in Dubai by Oriental Press

A catalogue record for this publication is available from the British Library

ISBN 978-1-107-61399-7 Reading and Writing 1 Student's Book with Online Workbook
ISBN 978-1-107-61401-7 Reading and Writing 1 Teacher's Book with DVD
ISBN 978-1-107-61399-7 Listening and Speaking 1 Student's Book with Online Workbook
ISBN 978-1-107-63461-9 Listening and Speaking 1 Teacher's Book with DVD

Additional resources for this publication at www.cambridge.org/unlock

Cambridge University Press has no responsibility for the persistence or accuracy of URLs for external or third-party internet websites referred to in this publication, and does not guarantee that any content on such websites is, or will remain, accurate or appropriate. Information regarding prices, travel timetables, and other factual information given in this work is correct at the time of first printing but Cambridge University Press does not guarantee the accuracy of such information thereafter.

It is normally necessary for written permission for copying to be obtained *in advance* from a publisher. The worksheets, role play cards, tests, and tapescripts at the back of this book are designed to be copied and distributed in class. The normal requirements are waived here and it is not necessary to write to Cambridge University Press for permission for an individual teacher to make copies for use within his or her own classroom. Only those pages that carry the wording '© Cambridge University Press' may be copied.

CALDERDALE
COLLEGE LIBRARY
HALIFAX

DATE 25-7-17
SOURCE Coutts
CLASS 428.24 OST
A/No. CCO46595/118965
PRICE £36.50

LC1

CONTENTS

5004770

UNL⊙CK UNIT STRUCTURE

The units in *Unlock Reading & Writing Skills* are carefully scaffolded so that students are taken step-by-step through the writing process.

UNLOCK YOUR KNOWLEDGE | Encourages discussion around the theme of the unit with inspiration from interesting questions and striking visuals.

WATCH AND LISTEN | Features an engaging and motivating *Discovery Education™* video which generates interest in the topic.

READING 1 | Practises the reading skills required to understand academic texts as well as the vocabulary needed to comprehend the text itself.

READING 2 | Presents a second text which provides a different angle on the topic in a different genre. It is a model text for the writing task.

LANGUAGE DEVELOPMENT | Practises the vocabulary and grammar from the Readings in preparation for the writing task.

CRITICAL THINKING | Contains brainstorming, evaluative and analytical tasks as preparation for the writing task.

GRAMMAR FOR WRITING | Presents and practises grammatical structures and features needed for the writing task.

ACADEMIC WRITING SKILLS | Practises all the writing skills needed for the writing task.

WRITING TASK | Uses the skills and language learnt over the course of the unit to draft and edit the writing task. Requires students to produce a piece of academic writing. Checklists help learners to edit their work.

OBJECTIVES REVIEW | Allows students to assess how well they have mastered the skills covered in the unit.

WORDLIST | Includes the key vocabulary from the unit.

This is the unit's main learning objective. It gives learners the opportunity to use all the language and skills they have learnt in the unit.

UNL⌀CK MOTIVATION

UNL⌀CK YOUR KNOWLEDGE • • • • • • • • •

Read the sentences (1–5) below and write the jobs from the box in the gaps. Use a dictionary to help you.

> architect   manager   software engineer
> nurse   primary school teacher

1 A _____ manages people.
2 An _____ designs buildings.
3 A _____ looks after people in a hospital.
4 A _____ manages software.
5 A _____ teaches young children.

PERSONALIZE

Unlock encourages students to bring their own knowledge, experiences and opinions to the topics. This motivates students to relate the topics to their own contexts.

DISCOVERY EDUCATION™ VIDEO

Thought-provoking videos from *Discovery Education*™ are included in every unit throughout the course to introduce topics, promote discussion and motivate learners. The videos provide a new angle on a wide range of academic subjects.

❝ The video was excellent! It helped with raising students' interest in the topic. It was well-structured and the language level was appropriate.

Maria Agata Szczerbik,
United Arab Emirates University,
Al-Ain, UAE ❞

UNLOCK CRITICAL THINKING

> The Critical thinking sections present a difficult area in an engaging and accessible way.
> Shirley Norton, London School of English, UK

BLOOM'S TAXONOMY

CREATE — create, invent, plan, compose, construct, design, imagine

decide, rate, choose, recommend, justify, assess, prioritize — **EVALUATE**

ANALYZE — explain, contrast, examine, identify, investigate, categorize

show, complete, use, classify, examine, illustrate, solve — **APPLY**

UNDERSTAND — compare, discuss, restate, predict, translate, outline

name, describe, relate, find, list, write, tell — **REMEMBER**

BLOOM'S TAXONOMY

The Critical Thinking sections in *Unlock* are based on Benjamin Bloom's classification of learning objectives. This ensures learners develop their **lower-** and **higher-order thinking skills**, ranging from demonstrating **knowledge** and **understanding** to in-depth **evaluation**.

The margin headings in the Critical Thinking sections highlight the exercises which develop Bloom's concepts.

LEARN TO THINK

Learners engage in **evaluative** and **analytical tasks** that are designed to ensure they do all of the thinking and information-gathering required for the end-of-unit writing task.

CRITICAL THINKING

UNDERSTAND

At the end of this unit, you will write facts. Look at this unit's writing task in the box below.

Write facts about the weather in your city.

EXPLANATION

Understand a table

A *table* shows facts and numbers. It is easy to see facts and numbers in a table.

Decimal numbers have a full stop in them – for example, 1.1, 1.7, 2.7. When we say decimal numbers, we use the word *point*.

1.1 *one point one*   1.7 *one point seven*   2.7 *two point seven*

Average temperatures and rainfall in Ulaanbaatar, Mongolia

month	average temperatures (°C)	average rainfall (mm)
January	−22	1.1
February	−16	1.7
March	−7	2.7

UNLOCK RESEARCH

THE CAMBRIDGE LEARNER CORPUS

The **Cambridge Learner Corpus** is a bank of official Cambridge English exam papers. Our exclusive access means we can use the corpus to carry out unique research and identify the most common errors learners make. That information is used to ensure the *Unlock* syllabus teaches the most **relevant language**.

THE WORDS YOU NEED

Language Development sections provide vocabulary and grammar building tasks that are further practised in the UNLOCK ONLINE Workbook. The glossary and end-of-unit wordlists provide definitions, pronunciation and handy summaries of all the key vocabulary.

PEOPLE   UNIT 1

⊙ LANGUAGE DEVELOPMENT

EXPLANATION

Nouns and verbs

Words for people, places or things are *nouns*. Words for states or actions are *verbs*. Sentences have nouns and verbs.

nouns: Tom is a doctor. He lives in New York. He works in a hospital.
verbs: Tom is a doctor. He lives in New York. He works in a hospital.

1 Read the sentences (1–7) and write the bold words in the correct places in the table below.

GRAMMAR FOR WRITING

EXPLANATION

The verb *be*

The verb *be* has three forms in the Present simple tense: *am*, *is*, *are*. After *I*, we use *am*. After *you*, *we* or *they*, we use *are*. After *he*, *she* or *it*, we use *is*.

I am a student.
You are a student. We are students. They are students.
Junko is a student. She is a student. My sister is a student.
Amir is a boxer. Sultan is a farmer. My grandfather is a doctor.
London is a big city. It is a big farm. His name is Tom.
Angela and Ottavio are Italian. They are Italian.

ACADEMIC LANGUAGE

Unique research using the **Cambridge English Corpus** has been carried out into academic language, in order to provide learners with relevant, academic vocabulary from the start (CEFR A1 and above). This addresses a gap in current academic vocabulary mapping and ensures learners are presented with carefully selected words they will find essential during their studies.

GRAMMAR FOR WRITING

The grammar syllabus is carefully designed to help learners become good writers of English. There is a strong focus on sentence structure, word agreement and referencing, which are important for **coherent** and **organized** academic writing.

> " The language development is clear and the strong lexical focus is positive as learners feel they make more progress when they learn more vocabulary.
> Colleen Wackrow,
> Princess Nourah Bint Abdulrahman University, Al-Riyadh, Kingdom of Saudi Arabia "

UNL⚙CK SOLUTIONS

FLEXIBLE

Unlock is available in a range of print and digital components, so teachers can mix and match according to their requirements.

UNL⚙CK ONLINE WORKBOOKS

The **⚙ UNLOCK ONLINE** Workbooks are accessed via activation codes packaged with the Student's Books. These **easy-to-use** workbooks provide interactive exercises, games, tasks, and further practice of the language and skills from the Student's Books in the Cambridge LMS, an engaging and modern learning environment.

CAMBRIDGE LEARNING MANAGEMENT SYSTEM (LMS)

The Cambridge LMS provides teachers with the ability to track learner progress and save valuable time thanks to automated marking functionality. Blogs, forums and other tools are also available to facilitate communication between students and teachers.

UNL⚙CK EBOOKS

The *Unlock* Student's Books and Teacher's Books are also available as interactive eBooks. With answers and *Discovery Education™* videos embedded, the eBooks provide a great alternative to the printed materials.

UNLOCK TEACHING TIPS

1 Using video in the classroom

The *Watch and listen* sections in *Unlock* are based on documentary-style videos from Discovery Education™. Each one provides a fresh angle on the unit topic and a stimulating lead-in to the unit.

There are many different ways of using the video in class. For example, you could use the video for free note-taking practice and ask learners to compare their notes to the video script; or you could ask learners to reconstruct the voiceover or record their own commentary to the video. Try not to interrupt the first viewing of a new video, you can go back and watch sections again or explain things for struggling learners. You can also watch with the subtitles turned on when the learners have done all the listening comprehension work required of them.

See also: Goldstein, B. and Driver, P. (2014) *Language Learning with Digital Video* Cambridge University Press and the *Unlock* website www.cambridge.org/unlock for more ideas on using video in the classroom.

2 Teaching reading skills

Learners who aim to study at university will need to be comfortable dealing with long, complex texts. The reading texts in *Unlock Reading & Writing Skills* provide learners with practice obtaining meaning quickly from extensive texts. Discourage your learners from reading every word of a text line-by-line and instead focus on skimming and scanning:

- Skimming – help promote quick and efficient reading. Ask learners to pass quickly over the text to get the basic gist, an awareness of the organization of the text and the tone and intention of the writer.

- Scanning – help learners locate key data and reject irrelevant information in a text. Ask learners to run their eyes up, down and diagonally (from left to right) across the text looking for clusters of important words. Search for names, places, people, dates, quantities, lists of nouns and compound adjectives.

The reading texts in *Unlock Reading & Writing Skills* demonstrate different genres such as academic text, magazine article or learner essay.

The *Reading between the lines* sections make learners aware of the different conventions of each genre. Understanding text genre should help prepare learners for the kind of content to expect in the text they are going to read. Ask learners to use *Reading 2* as a writing frame to plan their sentences, paragraphs and essays for the *Writing task*.

3 Managing discussions in the classroom

There are opportunities for discussion throughout *Unlock Reading & Writing Skills*. The photographs and the *Unlock your knowledge* boxes on the first page of each unit provide the first discussion opportunity. Learners could be asked to guess what is happening in the photographs or predict what is going to happen, for example. Learners could investigate the *Unlock your knowledge* questions for homework in preparation for the lesson.

Throughout the rest of the unit, the heading *Discussion* indicates a set of questions which can be an opportunity for free speaking practice. Learners can use these questions to develop their ideas about the topic and gain confidence in the arguments they will put forward in the *Writing task*.

To maximise speaking practice, learners could complete the discussion sections in pairs. Monitor each pair to check they can find enough to say and help where necessary. Encourage learners to minimise their use of their own language and make notes of any error correction and feedback after the learners have finished speaking.

An alternative approach might be to ask learners to role-play discussions in the character of one of the people in the unit. This may free the learners from the responsibility to provide the correct answer and allow them to see an argument from another perspective.

4 Teaching writing skills

Learners work towards the *Writing task* throughout the unit by learning vocabulary and grammar relevant for the *Writing task*, and then by reading about the key issues involved in the topic. Learners gather, organise and evaluate this information in the *Critical thinking* section and use it to prepare the *Writing task*. By the time learners come to attempt the *Writing task*, they have done all the thinking required to be able to write. They can do the *Writing task* during class time or for homework. If your learners require exam practice, set the writing task as a timed test with a minimum word count which is similar to the exam the learners are training for and do the writing task in exam conditions. Alternatively, allow learners to work together in the class to do the writing task and then set the *Additional writing task* (see below) in the Teacher's Book as homework.

Task and Language Checklists

Encourage your learners to edit their written work by referring to the *Task checklist* and *Language checklist* at the end of the unit.

Model answers

The model answers in the Teacher's Book can be used in a number of ways:

- Photocopy the *Writing task* model answer and hand this to your learners when you feedback on their writing task. You can highlight useful areas of language and discourse structure to help the learners compose a second draft or write a response to the additional writing tasks.

- Use the model answer as a teaching aid in class. Photocopy the answer and cut it up into paragraphs, sentences or lines then ask learners to order it correctly.

- Use a marker pen to delete academic vocabulary, key words or functional grammar. Ask learners to replace the missing words or phrases. Learners can test each other by gapping their own model answers which they swap with their partner.

Additional writing tasks

There are ten *Additional writing tasks* in the Teacher's Book, one for each unit. These provide another opportunity to practice the skills and language learnt in the unit. They can be handed out to learners or carried out on the Online Workbook.

5 Teaching vocabulary

The *Wordlist* at the end of each unit includes topic vocabulary and academic vocabulary. There are many ways that you can work with the vocabulary. During the early units, encourage the learners to learn the new words by setting regular review tests. You could ask the learners to choose e.g. five words from the unit vocabulary to learn. You could later test your learners' use of the words by asking them to write a short paragraph incorporating the words they have learned.

Use the end-of-unit *Wordlists* and the *Glossary* at the back of the book to give extra spelling practice. Set spelling tests at the end of every unit or dictate sets of words from the glossary which follow spelling patterns or contain common diagraphs (like *th, ch, sh, ph, wh*) or prefixes and suffixes (like *al-, in-, -tion, -ful*). You could also dictate a definition from the Glossary in English or provide the words in your learner's own language to make spelling tests more challenging.

6 Using the Research projects with your class

There is an opportunity for students to investigate and explore the unit topic further in the *Research projects* which feature at the end of each unit in the Teacher's Books. These are optional activities which will allow your learners to work in groups (or individually) to discover more about a particular aspect of the topic, carry out a problem-solving activity or engage in a task which takes their learning outside the classroom.

Learners can make use of the Cambridge LMS tools to share their work with the teacher or with the class as a whole. See section 5 above and section 8 on page 11 for more ideas.

7 Using UNLƆCK digital components: Online workbook and the Cambridge Learning Management System (LMS)

The Online Workbook provides:

- additional practice of the key skills and language covered in the Student's Book through interactive exercises. The **UNLƆCK ONLINE** symbol next to a section or activity in the Student's Book means that there is additional practice of that language or skill in the Online Workbook. These exercises are ideal as homework.

- End-of-unit *Writng tasks* and *Additional writing tasks* from the Teacher's Books. You can ask your learners to carry out both *writing tasks* in the Writing tool in the Online Workbook for homework. Then you can mark their written work and feed back to your learners online.

- a gradebook which allows you to track your learners' progress throughout the course. This can help structure a one-to-one review with the learner or be used as a record of learning. You can also use this to help you decide what to review in class.

- games for vocabulary and language practice which are not scored in the gradebook.

The Cambridge LMS provides the following tools:

- Blogs

The class blog can be used for free writing practice to consolidate learning and share ideas. For example, you could ask each learner to post a description of their holiday (or another event linked to a topic covered in class). You could ask them to read and comment on two other learners' posts.

- Forums

The forums can be used for discussions. You could post a discussion question (taken from the next lesson) and encourage learners to post their thoughts on the question for homework.

- Wikis

In each class there is a Wiki. You can set up pages within this. The wikis are ideal for whole class project work. You can use the wiki to practice process writing and to train the students to redraft and proof-read. Try not to correct students online. Take note of common errors and use these to create a fun activity to review the language in class. See www.cambridge.org/unlock for more ideas on using these tools with your class.

How to access the Cambridge LMS and setup classes

Go to **www.cambridge.org/unlock** for more information for teachers on accessing and using the Cambridge LMS and Online Workbooks.

---

8 Using *Unlock* interactive eBooks

Unlock Reading & Writing Skills Student's Books are available as fully interactive eBooks. The content of the printed Student's book and the Student's eBook is the same. However, there will be a number of differences in the way some content appears.

If you are using the interactive eBooks on tablet devices in the classroom, you may want to consider how this affects your class structure. For example, your learners will be able to independently access the video and audio content via the eBook. This means learners could do video activities at home and class time could be optimised on discussion activities and other productive tasks. Learners can compare their responses to the answer key in their eBooks which means the teacher may need to spend less time on checking answers with the whole class, leaving more time to monitor learner progress and help individual learners.

9 Using mobile technology in the language learning classroom

By Michael Pazinas, Curriculum and assessment coordinator for the Foundation Program at the United Arab Emirates University.

The presiding learning paradigm for mobile technology in the language classroom should be to create as many meaningful learning opportunities as possible for its users. What should be at the core of this thinking is that while modern mobile technology can be a 21st century 'super-toolbox', it should be there to support a larger learning strategy. Physical and virtual learning spaces, content and pedagogy all need to be factored in before deciding on delivery and ultimately the technological tools needed.

It is with these factors in mind, that the research projects featured in this Teacher's Book aim to add elements of hands-on inquiry, collaboration, critical thinking and analysis. They have real challenges, which learners have to research and find solutions for. In an ideal world, they can become tangible, important solutions. While they are designed with groups in mind, there is nothing to stop them being used with individuals. They can be fully enriching experiences, used as starting points or simply ideas to be adapted and streamlined. When used in these ways, learner devices can become research libraries, film, art and music studios, podcast stations, marketing offices and blog creation tools.

Michael has first-hand experience of developing materials for the paperless classroom. He is the author of the Research projects which feature in the Teacher's Books.

1 PEOPLE

Learning objectives

Go through the learning objectives with the class to make sure everyone understands what they can expect to achieve in this unit. Point out that learners will have a chance to review these objectives again at the end of the unit.

UNLOCK YOUR KNOWLEDGE

Lead-in

Show learners photos of people doing different jobs (e.g. from the Internet) and elicit words for as many different jobs as learners can think of. Write the words on the board. Elicit sentences about family members / friends and their jobs,
e.g. *My brother is a doctor*, etc.

👥 Focus on the questions. Learners ask and answer the questions with a partner. At the end, ask a few pairs to tell the class what they have learnt about their partner.

WATCH AND LISTEN

Optional activity

Focus on the video stills at the top of the page and ask learners to say what they can see. Ask: *What do you think these people's jobs are?*

PREPARING TO WATCH

UNDERSTANDING KEY VOCABULARY

Check that learners understand the meaning of the adjective *key* (= very important) in this heading.

1 👥 Explain that the places listed here are mentioned in the video learners are going to watch. Use a world map to make sure learners know where the countries are. Elicit the correct place number (5 *Milan*) for country **a** *Italy* from the class. Learners work in pairs to match the remaining places to the correct countries. Check answers with the class and

model and drill the pronunciation of *peninsula* /pəˈnɪnsjʊlə/. Ask: *Have you visited any of these places/countries?*

Answers

a 5 (Milan) b 3 (The Cape Peninsula) c 2 (New York)
d 6 (Mexico City) e 1 (New Delhi) f 4 (Cairo)

WHILE WATCHING

LISTENING FOR KEY INFORMATION

2 ▶ 👥 Go through the table with the class. Give the pronunciation of the names and elicit the meanings of *magazine* and *wedding*. Ask: *What's Sebastian's job? / What does Sebastian do?* (He is an artist.) *Where does Amarel work?* (New York) Write *fashion designer* /ˈfæʃən dɪˈzaɪnə/ and *fisherman* /ˈfɪʃəmən/ on the board and model the pronunciation of these. Play the video so that learners can complete the table. (You may need to play it more than once.) Point out that learners should write sentences like the models in the *job* column (these sentences are given in the video). After viewing, allow learners to discuss their answers in pairs before checking with the class. Keep explanations brief as learners will view the video again.

Answers

Amarel: She is a teacher.
Sebastian: Mexico City, Mexico
Angela: She is a famous fashion designer.
Yasmine: Cairo, Egypt
David: He is a fisherman.
Geeta: New Delhi, India

Video script

In this video, and in the course, you meet people from many different countries. You learn about their jobs and their families.

In the United States ...
Amarel works in New York. She is a teacher.
Amarel helps the children with their work and she asks them lots of questions. The children show Amarel what they are doing.

In Mexico ...
Sebastian is an artist.

Sebastian is famous in Mexico. His art is important. You can see some very large pieces of Sebastian's art in Mexico City.

In Italy …
Angela Missoni lives in Milan.
She is a famous fashion designer and she works with her family.
They make beautiful clothes.

In Egypt …
Yasmine lives in Cairo where she works for a fashion magazine.
She talks on the phone to journalists every day.
She enjoys her job. Yasmine lives with her mother and grandmother. They help her with the magazine.

In South Africa …
David lives on the Cape Peninsula.
He is a fisherman.
David catches fish every day and he teaches his sons how to fish.

In India …
Geeta lives in New Delhi.
She plans weddings. Geeta plans 500 weddings a year.
Three hundred people work for Geeta.

The people in this video speak different languages and do different jobs. But they all have one thing in common: they all have interesting lives.

3 ▶ ｊ Focus on the word box and the gapped sentences. Play the video again. Learners complete the sentences with the words from the box. Check answers with the class and model and drill the pronunciation of any difficult words, e.g. *beautiful* /ˈbjuːtɪfəl/, *interesting* /ˈɪntrəstɪŋ/, *different* /ˈdɪfrənt/, *famous* /ˈfeɪməs/.

| Answers
1 different 2 famous 3 beautiful 4 interesting

DISCUSSION

4 Focus on the questions and give learners a minute to think about their answers. (Question 3 could refer to the places featured in the video or any other countries learners may want to visit in the future.) Learners ask and answer the questions in pairs. Monitor, noting any common errors for future revision. Conduct full class feedback, commenting on what learners say (content) as well as paying particular attention to how they use the new vocabulary from the lesson and any issues with meaning or pronunciation. If you have time, you could get learners to change partners after feedback, to provide them with another opportunity to develop fluency and confidence.

READING 1
PREPARING TO READ
PREVIEWING

1 Previewing means looking at the main headings, style, photographs and layout of the text to predict or deduce its content and its origins. During this stage, learners will also draw on their existing knowledge of styles of text. Ask the questions before learners look at the text in order to give the previewing a purpose. Check answers with the class. You could ask learners if they use similar sites and, if appropriate, discuss the dangers of sharing too much personal information online with people who are not friends or family.

| Answers
1 b 2 c

Background note

This course has been designed to include a range of genres of text. In this unit, the text is a personal profile web page from an online social networking site which enables users to find friends and keep up-to-date with friends and family. The information is usually given in a fixed format under headings, e.g. *My life, My hobbies and interests*, etc.

Language note

A lot of the information in the profile is expressed through nouns: common nouns (e.g. *boxer, swimming*) and proper nouns (e.g. *Amir, Bolton Wanderers*). The Present simple is used to make general statements of fact, e.g. *I am, I speak, I like*, etc. The Present perfect is used to describe experience (*I have won many boxing matches*).

UNDERSTANDING KEY VOCABULARY

2 Focus on the word box and the gapped sentences. Ask learners to use a dictionary to help them complete the sentences with the words from the box. Check answers with the class and model and drill pronunciation of any difficult words, e.g. *language* /ˈlæŋgwɪdʒ/, *country* /ˈkʌntri/ and *birth* /bɜːθ/. Check understanding of the answers by eliciting more sentences using the words, e.g. *How many languages do you speak? What is your date of birth?* etc.

Answers

1 city 2 languages 3 country 4 birth

WHILE READING

SKIMMING

3 👤 Elicit the word *sportsman* by giving some examples of well-known sportsmen and asking learners: *What do we call a man who plays sport?* Focus on the headings in the box and elicit/pre-teach the meanings of *hobby* and *interest* here. (Check learners understand the meaning of *address*; here it means *email address*.) Learners skim the text to find the correct places for the headings. To ensure they skim the text (i.e. glance quickly at key words to gain a general understanding of what each section is about), set the task up carefully. Ask what information they are looking for (e.g. for *My hobbies and interests*, they are looking for examples of these). Ask: *Do you need to understand every word of the text to do this exercise?* (No). *How long will it take to do this?* (A short time). If you allow too much time, learners will begin to read the text in detail rather than skimming. Set/negotiate a time limit of one minute maximum. Check answers with the class.

Answers

1 My address 2 My family 3 My hobbies and interests 4 My life

SCANNING TO FIND INFORMATION

4 👤 To ensure learners scan the text (i.e. read quickly to pick out specific information), set the task up by completing the first sentence with the class. Ask which sections of the text and which words they need to look for to find the answer. Note that the word they need to look for may not always be one of the options in the sentences, although looking for these will help learners locate the information. (For example, for sentence 1, it would be quicker to look for 'Country' to find Amir Khan's own country of origin because 'Pakistan' will give them information about his parents' origins.)

Learners scan the text and choose the correct options for the remaining sentences. Check answers with the class. With a stronger class, you could point out the use of synonyms, e.g. *club* in the text but *team* in sentence 8; with weaker learners suggest that they look for the words from the sentence that are the same in the text, but to read around the text they find carefully.

Answers

1 the United Kingdom 2 boxer 3 swimming and football 4 sportsman 5 mother 6 father 7 info@amirsfans.co.uk 8 Bolton Wanderers

> ### Optional activity
>
> You could encourage learners to scan the text quickly by turning this activity into a race. Make sure learners start at the same time and ask them to close their books as soon as they have found all the correct options. Make a note of the first three or four finishers. Check the first finishers' answers. The first finisher with all the correct answers is the winner.

5 👤 Ask learners to read the summary and choose the correct words. They should try to do this without referring back to the personal profile as far as possible. Check answers with the class.

Answers

1 boxer 2 Bolton 3 1986 4 Haroon 5 Shah Khan

DISCUSSION

6 👥 You could demonstrate this activity first by asking a stronger learner the questions with the rest of the class listening. If necessary, explain the meaning of *How tall are you?* Learners then ask and answer the questions in pairs. Finish by asking one or two learners to tell the class what they have learned about their partner.

Use these additional questions to extend the discussion for stronger learners / fast finishers:

> *What are your hobbies?*
> *What is your favourite football club?*
> *Who is your favourite sportsman/ sportswoman?*

READING 2

Background note

The Reading 2 text is from a book of world records. World records give information about superlative human achievements (the fastest, tallest, fattest, best, etc.) as well as extremes in the natural world. For examples on the Internet, search for either the *Guinness World Records* or *RecordSetter* websites.

Turkey, officially the Republic of Turkey, is a Eurasian country, located mainly in western Asia but also southeastern Europe. The population is approximately 73.6 million and the country's official language is Turkish.

PREPARING TO READ

PREVIEWING

1 ▮ Focus on the *Previewing* box and go through the questions that can help us predict what a text is about. Explain that doing this can help us understand a text better when we read it in more detail. Learners look at the photographs and the text to find the correct endings for the statements. Learners can discuss the answers in pairs but should not start reading the text in detail. Check answers with the class.

Answers

1 b 2 c 3 a

UNDERSTANDING KEY VOCABULARY

2 ▮ Learners read the sentences and use the glossary on page 194 to help them understand the words in bold. Check learners' understanding by asking them personalized questions using the new vocabulary, e.g. *How tall are you? (I'm … cm tall.) My height* /haɪt/ *is … . Where do you live? Where does a doctor work? etc.* Model and drill the pronunciation of *clothes* /kləʊðz/ and *shoes* /ʃuːz/.

Optional activity

Ask learners to write sentences using the new vocabulary. Fast finishers could write a couple of gap-fill sentences for a partner to complete with the missing new words.

WHILE READING

SCANNING TO FIND INFORMATION

3 ▮ Revise the meaning of 'scanning' (i.e. letting the eyes move quickly over a text to find specific information). Focus on the profile which summarizes information from the reading text. Ask learners how they will read the text to find the correct options (quickly). Ask them if they need to understand every word or find particular words (find particular words). Set a time limit between 30 seconds and one minute. Check answers with the class. Ask: *Do you know any very tall people? Are there any tall people in your family? How tall are they?*

Answers

1 Sultan 2 Kösen 3 Turkey 4 Mardin
5 1982 (Note: this is answered through deduction rather than by finding this date in the text.)
6 one sister and three brothers 7 251 cm

4 ▮ Learners read the text again more slowly, then complete the sentences using words from the text. Complete the first sentence with the class, then learners can work individually. Check answers with the class.

Answers

1 is 2 lives 3 family 4 is 5 is 6 speaks

DISCUSSION

5 ▮ Learners discuss the questions in pairs. For feedback, ask one or two learners to tell the class about their partner or themselves. (Note that learners can just give a general location rather than giving the class their exact address for question 1.) Extend the discussion for fast finishers by giving them extra questions: *What does your brother/sister do ?/ What is your brother/sister's job? How well do you speak English/Arabic?*

◉ LANGUAGE DEVELOPMENT

Nouns and verbs

1 ▮ Go through the *Nouns and verbs* explanation box. Ask: *Which words are for people, places and things?* (nouns). *Which words are for states or actions?* (verbs; see

Language note). Focus on the table and elicit the first answer. Learners complete the exercise individually. Check answers with the class by getting learners to complete the table on the board.

Answers

nouns: Italy, brother, boxer, clothes, shoes
verbs: lives, works, is

> **Language note**
>
> A verb describing a state (e.g. *be*, *have* [for possession], etc.) gives a general fact about something or someone, e.g. *He **is** a doctor; She **has** a sister.* A verb describing an action describes something that happens or what someone does, e.g. *He **works** in Sharjah.*

> **Optional activity**
>
> Divide the class into teams. Say a word (i.e. either a verb or a noun) from the unit (plus a few others, e.g. *is, has*). The first team to correctly identify the form by calling out 'noun' or 'verb' wins a point.

Singular and plural nouns

2 Focus on the *Singular and plural nouns* explanation box and the regular plural form *-s*. (If you have time and your learners are ready for them, you could go through the irregular plural spellings given in the Language note below with the class.) Elicit the first answer from the class. Learners complete the exercise individually, then check with a partner. Check answers with the class.

Answers

1 sisters 2 pen 3 car 4 houses 5 cats

> **Language note**
>
> Other plural spelling patterns:
>
> For words ending in *s, sh, ch, x*, add *es*: *bus → buses, dish → dishes*.
>
> For words ending in *y*, change *y* to *ies*: *baby → babies, dictionary → dictionaries*
> but for words ending in *ay, ey, oy*, just add *s*: *day → days, key → keys*.
>
> For words ending in *f* or *fe*, change *f* to *ves*: *thief → thieves, knife → knives*.
>
> Irregular plurals:
>
> | | | |
> |---|---|---|
> | man → men | child → children | foot → feet |
> | tooth → teeth | woman → women | mouse → mice |
> | sheep → sheep | fish → fish | person → people |

3 Focus on the wordbox and the gapped sentences. Complete the first gap with the class. Learners complete the rest of the exercise individually then check in pairs. Check answers with the class.

Answers

1 is 2 teachers 3 speaks 4 brothers 5 lives
6 Rome

FAMILY VOCABULARY

4 As a lead-in to this exercise, you could draw your own family tree (or an invented one) on the board, including three generations with their names. Ask learners to give you the correct word for each family member and write it on the board next to their name (i.e. elicit *mother, father, brother, sister, grandmother, grandfather, uncle, aunt, son* and *daughter*).

Focus on the table and elicit the meanings of *male* and *female*. (Learners should be able to deduce these from the examples already in the table.) Complete the first gap with the class. Learners complete the remaining gaps individually, then check in pairs. Draw or project the table onto the board and check answers with the class.

Answers

1 grandfather 2 mother 3 daughter 4 brother
5 uncle

> **Optional activity**
>
> You could practise family vocabulary with a choral drill. First, read the prompts below out loud and ask learners to complete them with the correct word. Once they are familiar with the meaning and pronunciation, start the choral drill. Say the first sentence aloud (including the word in brackets) with a natural rhythm and ask the learners to repeat it together, copying your voice as closely as possible. After you have gone through the drill once or twice, vary it by asking half the class to repeat the first sentence and the other half to repeat the second sentence, etc.
>
> *My father's father is my … (grandfather)* /ˈgrændfɑːðə/
> *My father's mother is my … (grandmother)* /ˈgrændmʌðə/
> *My mother's sister is my … (aunt)* /ɑːnt/
> *My mother's brother is my … (uncle)* /ˈʌŋkl/
> *My mother's daughter is my … (sister)* /ˈsɪstə/
> *My mother's son is my … (brother)* /ˈbrʌðə/

CRITICAL THINKING

Go through the instructions with the class and focus on the writing task. Explain that the following sections of the unit will help them to prepare to write descriptive sentences about somebody in their family.

UNDERSTAND

1 👥 If you drew your own family tree on the board for Exercise 4 above, you could use it again to lead into the next activity. Ask questions about your family tree, e.g. *Who is …'s brother? Who is …'s mother? Who is …'s grandmother?* etc.

Focus on the family tree on page 25. Nominate learners to ask and answer the first one or two questions in open pairs. (If necessary, check understanding of the meaning of the possessive *'s* in every question, i.e. *Samira's brother = the brother of Samira*. The possessive *'s* tells us whose brother we are talking about.) Learners ask and answer the remaining questions in closed pairs. Monitor and only intervene if there is a breakdown in communication. Check answers with the class.

> **Answers**
>
> 1 Khaled 2 Samira 3 Laila 4 Samira and Alia
> 5 Samira and Alia 6 Abdullah 7 Khalifa 8 Samira and Alia

CREATE

2 and 3 👥 Ask learners to draw their own family trees. Go round the class and help as necessary. When they have finished, pairs ask and answer questions about each other's family trees, using the questions in Exercise 1 as models.

WRITING

GRAMMAR FOR WRITING

The verb *be*

Focus on the explanation box. Highlight the different forms of the verb *be* and the corresponding singular and plural pronouns (*I + am; you/we/they + are; he/she/it + is*). Point out the use of *is* and *are* after nouns, pronouns and proper nouns in the examples.

> **Language note**
>
> The Present simple form of *be* is used in key sentences that learners will need for the writing task. For example:
>
> 1 *am/is/are + from +* place name to say where someone is from.
> 2 *am/is +* number to say age.
> 3 *am/is + a +* profession (*are +* profession [plural]) (Note the use of the indefinite article in singular statements.)
> 4 *am/is/are +* nationality adjective.
>
> Use of the verb *to be* in these kinds of sentences may be difficult for some learners as some languages do not use a form of *be*, just two nouns together.

1 👤👥 Focus on the two gapped texts and complete the first gap with the class. Learners complete the remaining gaps individually, then check in pairs. If possible, project the texts onto the board to check answers with the class.

> **Answers**
>
> A
> 1 is 2 am 3 am 4 is
> 5 is 6 is 7 is 8 is
>
> B
> 1 am 2 am 3 is 4 are
> 5 is 6 is 7 is 8 are

Personal pronouns

2 👤 Focus on the *Personal pronouns* explanation box. Show how these personal subject pronouns link back to the preceding nouns in the example sentences by drawing arrows between them (written or projected onto the board). (If your class need extra help with or revision of personal subject pronouns, write the examples from the Language note on the board and highlight their use. You can also use this to look at/ revise object pronouns.)

Focus on the table and elicit the correct places in the table for the first one or two words from the wordbox. Learners complete the table with the remaining words from the box. Monitor and help as necessary. Check answers with the class.

> **Answers**
>
> she: mother, daughter
> he: grandfather, brother, father
> they: sons, aunts, uncles, sisters

Language note
Personal pronouns

Subject pronouns	Object pronouns
I	me
you	you
he	him
she	her
it	it
we	us
you	you
they	them

Personal subject pronouns

I like apples.
You (singular) like apples.

He likes apples. (masculine singular)
She likes apples. (feminine singular)
It likes apples. (**It** is used for objects, e.g. things and places, and often for animals.)

We like apples.
You (plural) like apples.
They like apples. (masculine and feminine plural)

Optional activity

Depending on your learners and their current knowledge, you could take this opportunity to teach or revise subject and object pronouns. Draw the table below on the board, omitting the pronouns and the sentences so that they can be added when learners give them. Elicit the subject and object pronouns from learners and write these in the table. Using the prompt like Faisal (or like Jin-young or a popular name from your teaching context), elicit the entences for the subject pronoun half of the table. (Note that you need to change the wording slightly for it.) When complete, you can model and drill these: say each sentence naturally and ask the class to repeat it. Then, using the same name and the verb, elicit the sentences for the object pronoun half of the table. (Again, you need to change the wording slightly for *it*.) Model and drill these sentences. Once learners are familiar with the form, vary it by asking half the class to repeat the first sentence and the other half to repeat the second sentence, e.g. A: *I like Faisal.* B: *Faisal likes me.*

Subject pronouns		Object pronouns	
I	I like Faisal.	Faisal likes **me**.	**me**
you	You like Jin-young.	Jin-young likes **you**.	**you**
he	He likes Faisal.	Faisal likes **him**.	**him**
she	She likes Jin-young.	Jin-young likes **her**.	**her**
it	Football is a sport. **It** is popular.	I like **it**.	**it**
we	We like Faisal.	Faisal likes **us**.	**us**
they	They like Jin-young.	Jin-young likes **them**.	**them**

3 👤 Focus on the subject pronouns in the box and the gapped sentences and elicit the first answer from the class. Ask why learners chose this answer (*she*), i.e. because the subject that *she* refers back to (*my sister*) is singular and female. Learners complete the remaining gaps. If learners need help, tell them to look at the verb form (singular or plural) after each gap. Check answers with the class.

> **Answers**
> 1 She 2 They 3 He 4 It

Possessive determiners

4 👤 Focus on the *Possessive determiners* explanation box and go through it with learners. (If your learners need revision here, use the tables from the Language note below; you could write the subject pronouns on the board and elicit the matching possessive determiners.) Focus on the possessive determiners in the wordbox in Exercise 4 and the gapped sentences and elicit the first answer from the class. Write the first completed answer on the board and show how *their* refers back to *two sisters* using an arrow. Learners complete the remaining sentences with the correct determiners. Check answers with the class. Copy or project the other sentences onto the board and show how the determiners link back to the preceding subjects.

> **Answers**
> 1 Their 2 Her 3 Our 4 My 5 His

Language note

Possessive determiners 'determine' or specify which noun is being referred to. They show possession or similar ideas. Note that it is the person or thing that owns something which affects which possessive determiner (masculine or feminine; singular or plural) is used; the thing that is owned does not affect which determiner is used, as in some languages. Watch out for confusion between *its* (i.e. belonging to it, as in *its eyes*) and *it's* (= it is, as in *It's blue*.).

Subject pronoun	Possessive determiner
I	my
you (singular)	your
he	his
she	her
it	its
we	our
you (plural)	your
they	their

> **Optional activity**
>
> Collect items from learners (e.g. pens, books, etc.). Use these to elicit sentences containing possessive determiners from the class, e.g. *Whose pen/book? His pen. My book. Her phone. Their pens. Our classroom.*

ACADEMIC WRITING SKILLS

Punctuation

Elicit the meanings of *capital letter* and *full stop* by asking a learner to write examples on the board. Ask learners to read the information in the box. You could write or project the example sentence on the board and highlight the capital letter at the beginning and full stop at the end. Point out that the remaining words in the sentence do not have a capital letter. Focus on the three other uses of an initial capital letter for names of people, places and for the first person subject pronoun.

> **Language note**
>
> An initial capital is always used for proper nouns (names). Most proper nouns do not have an article but there are exceptions (see Unit 4).

1 Focus on the first jumbled sentence and elicit the answer from the whole class. Draw attention to the capital letter at the beginning and the full stop at the end. Learners write the correct versions of the remaining sentences. Check answers with the class. Ask: *Who is 'He' in sentences 2–6?* (Zhong Shan).

> **Answers**
>
> 1 My grandfather is Zhong Shan.
> 2 He is 59.
> 3 He is a doctor.
> 4 He is from Hong Kong.
> 5 He has two daughters.
> 6 He lives with my mother and father.

2 Write or project the first sentence onto the board and make the corrections with the whole class. Learners correct the remaining sentences. Check answers with the class using the board.

> **Answers**
>
> 1 My name is Mohammed.
> 2 I am from Kuwait.
> 3 I am 19.
> 4 My father's name is Asif.
> 5 He is a teacher.
> 6 He has two sons.
> 7 My brother's name is Faran.
> 8 Faran is a doctor.
> 9 He lives in Canada.
> 10 Faran's hobbies are swimming and watching TV.

WRITING TASK

PLAN

1 and 2 Focus on the family tree learners drew in the previous lesson and ask them to choose one family member to write about. Copy or project the profile form onto the board and model filling it in for your own family member / an invented person, talking about the information as you do so, e.g. *His first name is Tom. His last name is Green*, etc. Ask learners to complete the profile for their family member.

WRITE A FIRST DRAFT

3 Focus on the table and show learners how to use it by making some sentences together. Using the information from their profile, learners write similar sentences about the family member they have chosen. Encourage learners to refer to the sentence patterns in the table when writing their own sentences, as these will help them with word order and use of pronouns.

EDIT

4 and 5 Focus on the task checklist. Go through the checklist together to make sure learners know what to check. Then ask learners to edit their sentences, using the checklist to help them. When they have checked and revised their writing, they can hand it in to you for marking. If the writing task has produced some common errors, you can look at these in the next lesson and use the model answer to highlight any particular areas.

> **Answers**
>
> See page 130 for a model answer.

Optional activity

After marking, you could ask learners to write a final neat version of their work for display in the classroom. You could also ask learners to identify similarities and differences between their own work and the Writing task model answer and the Hamdan and Min Lee texts on Student's Book page 26. Ask learners to underline/circle/highlight using coloured pens, etc., different examples of language from the unit (e.g. forms of *be*, nouns, verbs, pronouns or determiners) in both their work and the models.

OBJECTIVES REVIEW

See Introduction, page 9, for ideas about using the Objectives Review with your learners.

WORDLIST

See Introduction, page 9, for ideas about how to make the most of the Wordlist with your learners.

REVIEW TEST

See page 99 for the photocopiable Review Test for this unit and page 94, for ideas about when and how to administer the Review Test.

RESEARCH PROJECT

Set up a global people profile wiki.

Divide the class into groups and ask them to pick a country from around the world. Tell them not to choose the same country as another group. Also tell them that they have to find out about the people of that country by researching the information on the internet. They then have to come up with a wiki which gives the typical profile of someone from that country.

Allow the learners collaborate to build their own wiki. They can add as many or as few elements as they want.

2 SEASONS

Learning objectives

Go through the learning objectives with the class to make sure everyone understands what they can expect to achieve in this unit. Point out that learners will have a chance to review these objectives again at the end of the unit.

UNLOCK YOUR KNOWLEDGE

Lead-in

Ask: *What's the weather today? Is it hot/cold/sunny/rainy?* Show the class newspaper or Internet weather forecasts and look at the weather symbols for your city and other cities. Elicit what the symbols mean. Pre-teach the following vocabulary: *hot, warm, cold, sunny, windy, rainy, cloudy* (and any others that are useful for your teaching context).

Go through the words in the wordbox and check that learners understand them. Model and drill pronunciation if necessary, e.g. *autumn* /ˈɔːtəm/, *monsoon* /mɒnˈsuːn/. Ask: *What season is it here / in your country now?* Focus on the questions. Learners discuss the questions in pairs. Elicit feedback from a few pairs and discuss with the whole class.

WATCH AND LISTEN

Optional activity

Focus on the video stills at the top of the page and ask learners to say what they can see.

PREPARING TO WATCH

UNDERSTANDING KEY VOCABULARY

1 Focus on the wordbox and the photographs. Learners match the words to the correct photographs. Check answers with the class. Ask: *Does it snow much here / in your country?*

Answers

1 a snowflake 2 snow 3 a snowstorm

WHILE WATCHING

USING VISUALS TO PREDICT CONTENT

2 Play the first part of the video. Learners listen and circle the correct option (a–c). Check the answer with the class. Ask: *Have you ever been in a blizzard?*

Answer

b A blizzard is a kind of storm.

Video script

The northwest of the United States is an area with tall mountains and thick forests. The air is cold and so there is snow – a lot of snow! Up to about 15 metres a year. And when it is windy, the snow becomes a blizzard. A blizzard is a snowstorm with very strong winds.

In a blizzard, there is snow everywhere – in the cities, in the country and on the roads. A blizzard is very dangerous. Many roads close. When roads are open, drivers can't see. A blizzard can last for three hours and it is very cold. The temperature falls to minus 12 degrees Celsius.

The big, white cloud you can see here is a storm. It is going toward the northwest of the United States. In the cold air of the mountains, the storm becomes a blizzard. Snow begins to fall from the clouds.

Snow can be a big problem for people, like the driver of this car. Near the mountains and forest, there is more and more snow. He has a good car but it becomes stuck in the thick snow. He leaves the car and tries to walk. But it is cold and he is far from the city. He goes back to his car. The car is a safe place. There are tomatoes to eat and water to drink. The car is cold but he can turn on the engine to keep warm. Every day, he cleans snow from the car so people can see him. This blizzard lasts for 15 days. Finally, a policeman sees the car. The driver is saved!

UNDERSTANDING DETAIL

3 Focus on the wordbox and the gapped sentences. Learners complete the sentences with the correct words.

4 Play the first part of the video again so that learners can check their answers to Exercise 3. Check answers with the class.

Answers

1 cold 2 tall; forests 3 snow 4 winds 5 dangerous
6 close 7 see

5 ▶ 👤👥 Play the next part of the video. Learners watch, then mark the statements true or false. Learners check their answers in pairs. Check answers with the class and elicit the correct versions of the false sentences.

> **Answers**
> 1 F The big white cloud is a storm.
> 2 T
> 3 F The man's car is good.
> 4 F The car is far from the city.
> 5 F He eats tomatoes.
> 6 T

DISCUSSION

6 👥 Pairs of learners decide who is student A and who is B, then ask and answer the questions. Learners can use information they remember from the video as well as their answers to Exercise 5. Elicit feedback from one or two pairs.

READING 1

PREPARING TO READ

UNDERSTANDING KEY VOCABULARY

1 👤 You could lead in to this exercise by writing the following sentences on the board and asking learners to find the two words with an opposite meaning:

> *My cousin is a very tall man.*
> *My father is short but strong.* (Answer: *tall* and *short*)

Learners match sentences 1–4 to sentences a–d using a dictionary if necessary, then check their answers in pairs. Check answers with the class. Model and drill the pronunciation of *minus* /ˈmaɪnəs/ and *warm* /wɔːm/. Write the plus and minus signs on the board and show how these signs can be used before numbers to show temperatures above and below freezing.

> **Answers**
> 1 d 2 c 3 a 4 b

2 👤👥 Learners match the full number words to the correct figures, then check their answers in pairs. Check answers with the class.

> **Answers**
> 1 e 2 f 3 b 4 a 5 d 6 c 7 g

PREVIEWING

3 👤👥 Remind learners of the previewing they did in Unit 1, i.e. looking at the layout, headings and visuals (photographs, illustrations, graphs, diagrams, etc.) in a text and using their knowledge and experience to decide what sort of text it is and the kind of information it will contain. Ask them to read the four statements before they start looking at this text and remind them to look only at the graph, photographs and headings to find the answers. (Check they understand the meaning of *heading* and *graph*.) Learners mark the statements true or false, then check their answers in pairs. Check answers with the class and elicit the correct versions of the false statements.

> **Answers**
> 1 T
> 2 T
> 3 F Summer is warm.
> 4 F Svetlana has a café in Yakutsk.

> **Background note**
>
> Russia, officially known as the Russian Federation, is a country in northern Eurasia. At 17 million square kilometres (6.6 million square miles), Russia is the largest country in the world. It is also the world's ninth most populated country with approximately 143 million people. Yakutsk is the capital city of the Sakha Republic in the east of Russia, located about 450 kilometres (280 miles) south of the Arctic Circle and approximately 8,300 kilometres (5,160 miles) from Moscow.

> **Language note**
>
> In the UK, a *kindergarten* /ˈkɪndəgaːtən/ is a school for children between the ages of two and five. In the US, a *kindergarten* /ˈkɪndərgaːrtn/ is a school or class that prepares five-year-old children for school.

4 👤 If possible, prepare a translation of the graph caption into your language before the lesson. You can compare this with your learners' translations when you check these with the class. Focus on the graph and its caption. Ask learners to translate it but not to use a dictionary or the Student's Book glossary at this stage.

Answers

Answers will vary.

5 👤 Learners check their translations using the Student's Book glossary. Discuss and agree on a correct translation with the class. Point out that *average* /ˈævərɪdʒ/ has a mathematical meaning and a more general meaning = *usual*. Model and drill the pronunciation of /ˈtemprətʃə/.

WHILE READING

SCANNING TO FIND INFORMATION

Ask learners to read the tips on what to look for when scanning a text in the *Scanning to find information* box. Point out that when scanning our eyes move quickly across the text, searching for certain kinds of words or information, rather than moving slowly and concentrating on every word.

6 👤👥 Focus on the facts (1–6) and the numbers (a–f). Elicit the meaning of °C (= degrees centigrade /ˈsentɪɡreɪd/ or *Celsius* /ˈselsiəs/). Ask learners which items they should scan for in the text (= the numbers and the names, e.g. *Yakutsk* and *Daria*). Match the first items together with the class as an example. Point out that learners can also use their existing knowledge as well as logical deduction to guess the figures which are likely to match each fact. Set a time limit to make sure that learners scan properly. Learners complete the rest of the exercise individually before checking their answers in pairs. Check answers with the class.

Answers

1 e 2 b 3 a 4 c 5 d 6 f

Background note

Centigrade (or *Celsius*) is a unit of measurement of temperature usually shown by the letter *C*. *Celsius* is named after the Swedish astronomer Anders Celsius (1701–1744).

DISCUSSION

7 👥 If you are short of time, ask learners to discuss the questions in pairs. For feedback, ask one or two learners to tell the class their or their partner's answers.

Optional activity

To extend the discussion, give learners time to prepare their responses to the questions in Exercise 7. You could also put them into new pairs or small groups. Suggest further questions and discussion points, e.g.:

What is the average summer temperature in your country?
What is the average winter temperature in your country?
Is life easier in the winter or the summer? Why?
Would you like to live in Yakutsk? Would you like to go there?

Set up a whole class discussion, letting the learners answer the questions as much as possible without your help. At the end, give praise and feedback on learners' ideas and language (consider both range and accuracy).

READING 2

PREPARING TO READ

PREVIEWING

1 👤 Ask learners what they need to look at when previewing a text (headings, photographs, diagrams, graphs, etc.). Focus learners on the questions. Set a time limit if necessary to make sure that learners answer the questions quickly rather than reading carefully and slowly. Learners answer the questions individually. Check answers with the class.

Answers

1 c 2 b 3 c

UNDERSTANDING KEY VOCABULARY

2 👤 Focus on the gapped sentences and the wordbox. Learners should use a dictionary complete the sentences. Check answers with the class. Highlight the ways of recording centigrade (°C) and measurements (*kph* = kilometres per hour and *mm* = millimetres). You could write some examples of these with different numbers on the board for learners to say aloud.

Answers

1 temperature 2 wind speed 3 rainfall 4 climate

3 🔒 Focus on Text B and the weather symbols used in it. Elicit the meaning of the symbol next to gap 1 and the correct word from the box (*cloudy*). Learners complete the remaining gaps, using a dictionary to help them. If possible, project Text B onto the board to check answers with the class. Ask: *What is the weather like today?* to elicit one of the new words.

> **Answers**
>
> 1 cloudy 2 rainy 3 sunny 4 windy

WHILE READING

> **Background note**
>
> The Caribbean consists of the sea which is east of Central America and north of South America as well as the islands and countries in and around the Caribbean Sea. The Caribbean islands, including Cuba, are popular holiday destinations. The main island of Cuba is the largest island in the Caribbean and has a population of approximately 11.2 million.

> **Language note**
>
> There are two possible ways to pronounce *Caribbean*: /ˌkærɪˈbiːən/ and /kəˈrɪbiən/, both of which are widely used and accepted in the US. In the Caribbean, the stress is put on the second syllable, /ˈrɪb/. Traditionally in the UK, the stress was on the third syllable /ˈbiː/ but the pronunciation used in the Caribbean has become increasingly popular.

SCANNING TO FIND INFORMATION

4 🔒👥 Focus on the facts and numbers/words. Remind learners of the scanning explanation box and the scanning they did for Reading 1. Elicit what they will need to look for in the text (numbers and names of months). Elicit the first answer from the class. Learners match the remaining items individually before checking in pairs. Check answers with the class.

> **Answers**
>
> 1 c 2 h 3 f 4 b 5 e 6 a 7 d 8 g

DISCUSSION

5 👥 If you are short of time, ask learners to discuss the questions in pairs. For feedback, ask one or two learners to tell the class

their answers. You could then open up the discussion to the whole class.

> **Answers**
>
> 1 Yes
> 2 The dry season and the rainy season
> 3 Answers will vary.
> 4 Answers will vary.
> 5 The Internet/Tourist Information Office/Guidebooks

> **Optional activity**
>
> To extend the discussion, give learners time to prepare their responses to the questions in Exercise 5. You could also put them into new pairs or small groups. For fast finishers / more able learners, you can suggest further questions and discussion points, e.g.:
>
> *Is the weather in Cuba good or bad for tourists? Why? / Why not?*
> *Is the weather in Cuba good for farmers? Why? / Why not?*
> *Is Cuba a good place for a holiday? Why? / Why not?*
> *Would you like to go there? Why? / Why not?*
> *Is the weather in your country good or bad for tourists? Why? /Why not?*
> *Is the weather in your country good or bad for farmers? Why? /Why not?*

⊙ LANGUAGE DEVELOPMENT

> **Optional activity**
>
> You could lead into this section by revising the new vocabulary in the unit so far. Dictate some nouns and adjectives for learners to write down, asking them to pay particular attention to spelling: e.g. *happy, easy, difficult, average, temperature, summer.*

Adjectives and nouns

1 🔒 Focus on the *Adjectives and nouns* explanation box and make sure learners understand the terms. If you started the lesson with the optional activity, you could ask the learners to sort those words into adjectives and nouns. Demonstrate the exercise by doing the first one together. Learners complete the exercise individually. Check answers with the class. For feedback, you could ask learners to circle and underline the answers on the board.

Answers

adjectives:
1 warm 2 difficult 3 good 4 hot 5 cold
nouns:
1 café 2 Life 3 climate 4 Summers 5 Winters

2 👤 To lead in to this exercise, you could briefly revise singular and plural nouns and highlight the forms of the verbs that follow them. Write singular and plural nouns on the board and elicit the correct form of *be* after each, e.g. *Summers … (are) hot. Life … (is) difficult.*

Learners read the sentences first, then complete the gaps using the words from the box. Check answers with the class.

Answers

1 is 2 are 3 sunny 4 weather 5 brother

Noun phrases

3 👤👥 Focus on the *Noun phrases* explanation box. Explain that a phrase is a group of words which is part of a sentence. Highlight the form and elicit further examples from learners. Complete the first sentence with the class. Learners complete the exercise individually, then check in pairs. Check answers with the class.

Answers

1 warm café 2 difficult life 3 good climate 4 warm summers

Language note

The adjective usually goes before the noun in a noun phrase in English, not after the noun as in many languages.

---

4 👥 Demonstrate Exercise 4 by doing the first answer together with the class. You could write or project the first sentence and show the correction on the board. Learners complete the exercise in pairs. (Note that in questions 4 and 5 there are two errors: misplaced adjectives and extra verbs.) Check answers with the class.

Answers

1 Cuba has a <u>good climate</u>.
2 I have a <u>happy family</u>.
3 In summer, we have <u>good weather</u>.
4 The <u>dry season is</u> from June to November.
5 The <u>average rainfall is</u> 78 mm in spring.

CRITICAL THINKING

Go through the instructions with the class and focus on the writing task. Explain that the following sections of the unit will help them to prepare and write factual sentences about the weather in their city.

UNDERSTAND

Focus on the *Understand a table* explanation box and point out the table showing temperatures and rainfall in Ulaanbaatar. Go through the form for writing decimal numbers and their pronunciation, asking learners to say some of the decimals aloud. Check the full form and pronunciation of 0 = *zero* /ˈzɪərəʊ/.

Optional activity

Write some decimal numbers on the board and ask learners to read them out. Dictate some other decimal numbers (randomly mixed together with whole numbers, plus and minus numbers and numbers with *mm* and *kph* abbreviations as revision) and ask learners to write them on their pads/the board. Check answers with the class.

Alternatively, this could be set up as a Bingo game. Write a selection of 12 different numbers (plus/minus ones, measurements and decimals) on the board. Ask learners to choose four of these and write them down. Read out the numbers from the board in random order. Learners cross off the numbers they have written when they hear them. The first learner to cross off all four of their numbers correctly is the winner.

---

1 👥 Focus learners on Table 3.4 and ask what information it shows (facts about the climate – average temperatures and rainfall – in Ulaanbaatar in Mongolia). Ask one or two simple questions to check learners' understanding, e.g. *What's the average temperature in March?* (minus 7) *What's the average rainfall in January?* (1.1 mm)

Nominate individual learners to ask and answer the first one or two questions across the class in open pairs. Encourage learners to develop their answers and give supporting reasons rather than just Yes/No answers to questions 1–4 so that they can practise saying the different numbers and abbreviations. For question 5, elicit which months are the summer months (June, July and August). Put learners in closed pairs. As pairs ask and answer the questions, monitor and only intervene if there is a breakdown in communication. Check answers with the class.

Answers

1 No (the average rainfall is 1.7 mm)
2 No (the average rainfall is 52 mm)
3 Yes (the average temperature is +2 °C)
4 Yes (the average temperature is 0 °C)
5 Summer is rainy.

APPLY

2 👤 Focus on the gapped text and ask learners to read it. Complete the first two gaps together with the class using information from Table 3.4. For gap 2, elicit or explain the meaning of *from … to …* to show a range from lowest to highest (*from –16 to –22*) or a period of time (*from December to February*). Learners complete the rest of the text. Check answers with the class. Ask: *Would you like to live in Ulaanbaatar? What do you think of the climate?*

Answers

1 Mongolia 2 –16 3 rainfall 4 1.1 5 temperatures
6 +19 7 average 8 42

Background note

Mongolia is a country in central and eastern Asia. The population is approximately 2.8 million and the country's official language is Mongolian. Ulaanbaatar is the capital and the largest city.

WRITING

GRAMMAR FOR WRITING

Subject and verb

Focus on the *Subject and verb* explanation box. Highlight the different forms that can be used as a subject. Elicit further examples of pronouns to revise these from Unit 1. Elicit other nouns and noun phrases. You could write other sentences on the board and ask learners to underline the subjects, e.g. *The average rainfall in Egypt (is 62 mm); The average temperature in the dry season is 30 degrees.* Point out the position of the verb after all the types of subject.

1 👤👥 Demonstrate the exercise by matching the first pair of sentence halves with the class. Remind learners to check whether the verb is singular or plural. Learners then match the remaining sentences individually, then check in pairs. Check answers with the class.

Answers

1 d 2 e 3 a 4 c 5 b

Prepositions

Focus on the *Prepositions* box. Explain that prepositions are used before a pronoun, noun or noun phrase to connect it to another word or part of a sentence, e.g. *I am going to Beijing.* Check learners understand the prepositions in the box and their use.

2 👤 Ask learners to complete the sentences with the correct prepositions from the box. Check answers with the class. You could also ask learners to refer back to the text about the weather in Ulaanbaatar on page 43 or project this text onto the board and refer to the original sentences there.

Answers

1 in 2 in 3 from, to 4 In, from, to 5 in

Optional activity

You could practise the use of *in* with other seasons/ cities and countries, and *from … to …* with months and with measurements (e.g. temperatures and rainfall) by asking learners to complete the following sentences (or use examples from your own teaching context). For example:

Paris is … (in France).
Summers are hot … (in Morocco).
In summer, the average temperatures in Marrakesh are … (from) +18 °C … (to) 37 °C.
In summer, the average rainfall in Marrakesh is … (from)
2 mm … (to) 7 mm.
In winter, the average rainfall in Paris is … (from) 46 mm … (to) 50 mm.

Prepositional phrases

Focus on the *Prepositional phrases* explanation box. Show that one type of prepositional phrase gives information about 'where' and the other type gives information about 'when'. Point out that *in* can be used to say both 'where' and 'when'. Revise the use of *be from* + city/country to talk about where you are from.

3 👤 Ask learners to circle the 'when' prepositional phrases in the two sentences. Check answers with the class.

Answers

1 In the dry season
2 in the dry season

4 Elicit the answer to the question. Point out that when the prepositional phrase is at the start of the sentence, it is followed by a comma. Ask learners what a comma shows (= a slight pause or a way of breaking up long chunks of text).

Answers

Sentence 1

5 🔲 Ask learners to complete the sentences using the prepositional phrases from the box. As the phrases could complete any of the sentences grammatically, they should think carefully about meaning and the most sensible places for them. Check answers with the class. Check punctuation by writing the answers on the board. Question 2 requires a capital letter on *In* and a comma because the prepositional phrase comes at the beginning of the sentence.

Answers

1 in winter 2 In July, 3 in the monsoon season

6 🔲 Demonstrate this exercise by doing the first one with the class. Learners should notice that if the jumbled words include a comma and if the preposition has a capital letter, this means that the prepositional phrase should come at the beginning of the sentence (with the comma after it). Check answers with the class.

Answers

1 In October, it is windy.
2 The weather is good in summer.
3 In Cuba, the climate is good.
4 In autumn, the average rainfall is 34 mm.
5 The winters are cold in Yakutsk.
6 The average temperature is 27 °C in the monsoon season.
7 In the dry season, the average rainfall is 7 mm.

Optional activity

Before the lesson, write each word in the first one or two sentences in Exercise 6 on separate large pieces of paper and ask a matching number of learners to stand in front of the class. Give each learner one word (or comma) to hold up and ask the rest of the class to tell their classmates to move into the right positions to show the correct sentence order.

ACADEMIC WRITING SKILLS

Spelling

1 🔲 Focus on the *Capital letters* box and elicit other examples for each category. Learners complete the months with the missing letters. Check answers with the class and highlight any difficult spellings, e.g. *February, August.*

Answers

J a n u a r y	J u l y
F e b r u a r y	A u g u s t
M a r c h	S e p t e m b e r
A p r i l	O c t o b e r
M a y	N o v e m b e r
J u n e	D e c e m b e r

2 🔲 Revise the use of an initial capital letter for the first word in a sentence and a full stop at the end (Unit 1).
Ask one (confident) learner to correct the first sentence on the board. Ask the class if the sentence is now correct; if it is not, ask another learner to make any other necessary corrections. If necessary, remind learners of the use of a comma after a prepositional phrase at the beginning of a sentence. Learners correct the remaining sentences. Check answers with the class.

Answers

1 In January, the weather is cold in Russia.
2 The average temperature is 21 °C in July.
3 In the monsoon season, the average rainfall is 315 mm in Bangalore in India.
4 The weather is sunny on Tuesday.
5 Sultan lives in Sharjah in the United Arab Emirates.

WRITING TASK

PLAN

1 🔲 Focus on the multiple choice options. Learners choose the correct option for their city.

2–5 🔲 Focus on the table and go through the columns and rows making sure learners understand the information they have to fill in. (You could fill in a model row on the board if necessary.) Learners complete two or more rows of the table (depending on the number of seasons their city has), using the Internet to find any information they need.

WRITE A FIRST DRAFT

6   Ask learners to look back at the Critical thinking section and read the text about Ulaanbaatar again. This text will provide a model for their own writing. Highlight the key language in this text: adjectives and nouns, noun phrases, subjects and verbs, prepositions (*in* + country/city, *in* + month/ season, *from … to…* + measurements/ months), etc.

7   Ask learners to complete the sentences with information about their city.

8   Learners use the prompts and the information they have included in the table in Exercise 2 to write sentences about the weather in their city. You could elicit/model an example for the first sentence, e.g. *In summer, it is very hot / It is very hot in summer*, and write this on the board. Ask learners to copy the first paragraph from Exercise 7 as their introduction and write the other sentences underneath. Monitor and help with any vocabulary they may need.

EDIT

9 and 10   Focus on the task checklist. Go through the checklist together to make sure the learners know what to check. Then ask learners to edit their sentences, using the checklist to help them. When they have checked and revised their writing, they can hand it in to you for marking. If the writing task has produced some common errors, you can look at these in the next lesson and use the model answer to highlight any particular areas.

> **Answers**
> See page 131 for a model answer.

Optional activity

Ask learners to identify similarities and differences between their own work and the Ulaanbaatar text on Student's Book page 43. Ask learners to pick out a particular example of language from the unit (e.g. adjectives, nouns, noun phrases, subjects and verbs or prepositions) in both their work and the Ulaanbaatar text and to mark these using different coloured pens or by underlining or circling them.

OBJECTIVES REVIEW

See Introduction, page 9, for ideas about using the Objectives Review with your learners.

WORDLIST

See Introduction, page 9, for ideas about how to make the most of the Wordlist with your learners.

REVIEW TEST

See page 94 for the photocopiable Review Test for this unit and page 102, for ideas about when and how to administer the Review Test.

RESEARCH PROJECT

Set up a weather station to monitor the weather.

Divide the class into teams asking them to research ways to monitor the weather. Tell them that they have to think about rainfall, temperature, wind speed and direction, and air pressure. Learners need to collaborate to find ways of acquiring the equipment or data they need. Learners can choose to acquire the data themselves manually. In this case, they will need to find out what apparatus they need and how they will use it to record the weather. Alternatively, learners can use the internet to access local weather data and compare weather data over a period of time with that from different countries or areas in the region.

The aim is to record the results of their project and write about them.

3 LIFESTYLE

Learning objectives

Go through the learning objectives with the class to make sure everyone understands what they can expect to achieve in this unit. Point out that learners will have a chance to review these objectives again at the end of the unit.

UNLOCK YOUR KNOWLEDGE

Lead-in

Ask learners about a typical working day in their country:
What time do people usually get up?
What time do they start/finish work?
When do they have breakfast/lunch/dinner?

👥 Put learners in pairs and get them to ask and answer similar questions for a typical student in their country. Monitor, then ask one pair to report back to the class. You could pre-teach *lecture* /ˈlektʃə/ (a formal talk on a serious or specialist subject given to a group of people, especially students), *seminar* /ˈsemɪnɑː/ (an occasion when a teacher or expert and a group of people meet to study and discuss something) and *timetable* /ˈtaɪmteɪbl̩/ (a list of the times when classes in school happen).

1 👤 Focus on the wordbox and the gapped phrases. Learners write the words in the correct gaps. Check answers with the class.

> **Answers**
>
> 1 relax with friends in a café
> 2 study in your room
> 3 work in a shop
> 4 work in an office

2 👥 Focus on the questions. Learners ask and answer with a partner. Ask one or two pairs to tell the class about their partner.

WATCH AND LISTEN

Optional activity

Focus on the video stills at the top of the page and ask learners to say what they can see.

PREPARING TO WATCH

UNDERSTANDING KEY VOCABULARY

1 👤 Focus on the diagram of a mine and pre-teach this word. Ask learners to check the meanings of the words in the diagram using a dictionary. Ask: *What does a miner do?* (He/she works in a mine.) *Where are mines?* (underground)

2 👤👥 Focus on the sentences and the words in the box. Complete the first sentence with the class as an example. Remind them to use the diagram to help them with the new vocabulary. Learners complete the remaining sentences, then check their answers in pairs. Check answers with the class. Ask: *Is there a desert / Are there mines in your country?*

> **Answers**
>
> 1 desert 2 dust 3 underground 4 rock 5 mine
> 6 comfortable

WHILE WATCHING

UNDERSTANDING MAIN IDEAS

3 👤 Focus on the statements in the table. Elicit/pre-teach the meanings of *opal* /ˈəʊpl̩/, *stone* and *golf* using the video stills and/or pictures from the Internet. Learners decide if the statements are true or false and write (T) or (F) in column A. Explain that some of their answers will be guesses at this point.

> **Answers**
>
> Answers will vary.

4 ▶️👤👥 Play the video. Learners watch, then complete column B in the table in Exercise 3. Allow learners to discuss their answers in pairs before checking answers with the class. You could elicit correct versions of the false sentences, e.g. *The people don't live in tall houses. They live underground.* Ask: *Did anything surprise you in the video? Do people play golf at night in your country / live in underground houses?*

Answers

1 T
2 F They live underground.
3 F The people are miners; they work in the mines.
4 T
5 T
6 T

Video script

Coober Pedy, South Australia

It is hot here. The average temperature can get as high as 55 degrees centigrade. How can people live here? The answer? They live underground. They make houses from the rock.

These houses are comfortable. Dust can be a problem. But the people vacuum every day. Almost 3,000 people live in houses like this one. But why do people live in Coober Pedy? They live here to work in the opal mines.

This is an opal. You can sell a good opal for 50,000 dollars! Ninety-five per cent of all opal in the world comes from Australia.

Milena Telak is from Croatia. She is an opal miner. Every day, Milena goes to work in her opal mine. She likes her job. She likes working underground. Milena works with other miners. They use big machines to cut the rock.

What do people in Coober Pedy do in their free time?

They play golf! It is too hot to play in the day so they play at night. They use bright green golf balls.

LISTENING FOR KEY INFORMATION

5 ▶️ 👤 Focus on the numbers in the box and elicit/model pronunciation of each number (*forty-two, fifty-five, ninety-five, three thousand, five thousand, fifty thousand*). Go through the facts to make sure learners understand them. Play the video again. Learners watch and write the numbers next to the correct facts. Remind them there are three numbers they do not need. Check answers with the class. Ask: *How much does a good opal cost?* (50,000 dollars); *How hot is it in the Australian desert?* (55 degrees centigrade/ Celsius); *How many people live in the town?* (3,000).

Answers

1 3,000 2 50,000 3 55

Background note

Opals are a precious multicoloured stone used in jewellery.

Coober Pedy is in South Australia, 846 kilometres (525 miles) north of Adelaide. It is sometimes called the 'opal capital of the world' because of the number of opals mined there. It is well known for its underground houses, called 'dugouts'. The name Coober Pedy means 'white man's hole' in the local Aboriginal language.

DISCUSSION

6 👥 Focus on the questions. Learners ask and answer in pairs. Monitor and make a note of any interesting points learners make. Conduct full class feedback and ask individual learners to share their ideas with the class. You could use this discussion to help learners produce more complex language, e.g. *I'd / I wouldn't like to live in Coober Pedy because …; I don't like the underground houses because …; Life is different from my town because … .*

Answers

Answers will vary.

READING 1

PREPARING TO READ

👥 To lead in to the reading text, ask learners to tell their partners about the last book they read and to say why they chose to read it. Elicit feedback from one or two pairs. Ask: *How do people choose books?* Elicit that there is often a short description plus reviews of a book (a *blurb*) on its back cover, which tries to persuade people to buy and read it. Look at real examples of back covers here, including those of the books the learners are using.

PREVIEWING

1 👤 Focus on the wordbox and the text. Ask learners to circle the words in the box if they can see any of the things listed, either on the book cover itself or in the photographs. To introduce a competitive element to this, you could set a time limit; the winner is the first learner to circle the correct words. Check answers with the class.

Answers

a writer, a hunter, a tree house, a price, a book cover, the name of a newspaper

UNDERSTANDING KEY VOCABULARY

2 👤 Focus on the sentences and the words in the box. Elicit the first answer from the class as an example. Learners read and complete the remaining sentences. Check answers with the class.

Answers

1 imagine 2 cook 3 traditional 4 lifestyle
5 different 6 hunt 7 jungle 8 amazing

WHILE READING

Background note

Papua New Guinea, officially the Independent State of Papua New Guinea, is in the southwestern Pacific Ocean. Papua New Guinea occupies the eastern part of the world's second largest island. The capital city is Port Moresby. Its population is approximately 7 million and the majority of the population (approximately 80 per cent) live in rural areas.

SCANNING TO FIND INFORMATION

3 👤 Check understanding of (or pre-teach) *meat* and *banana* using the Internet or photographs. Revise the scanning technique from the previous units if necessary. Focus on the completed example. Ask: *Who hunts animals in the jungle?* (Kombai men) Focus on the second row of the table, ask: *Who travels 15,000 kilometres?* and elicit the information learners will scan the text for (*15,000 km*) and the correct answer (Rebecca Moore). Learners scan the text to complete the rest of the table. Point out that for some questions (e.g. question 4) more than one column of the table will need a tick. As learners scan and complete the exercise, monitor and help as necessary. Check answers with the class.

Answers

	Rebecca Moore	Kombai men	Kombai women	Kombai children
1 hunt animals in the jungle		✓		
2 travels 15,000 km	✓			
3 cook			✓	
4 eat green bananas		✓	✓	✓
5 have no cars		✓	✓	✓
6 teach children the traditional lifestyle		✓	✓	
7 build tree houses		✓	✓	✓
8 tells the story of the traditional Kombai lifestyle	✓			

4 👤 Focus on the *Pronouns and possessive determiners* explanation box and highlight the ways in which pronouns and determiners refer back to nouns. Write the examples on the board and draw arrows to make the references clear and visual, e.g.:

Faisal has a new mobile phone. It is amazing.

Kamile has a new car. Her car is amazing.

Elicit the first answer to the exercise from the class as an example (1b). Show how *she* in sentence (b) refers back to *Rebecca* in sentence (1). Learners match the remaining sentences, using the personal pronouns to help them.

5 👤 Learners check their answers to Exercise 4 by reading the text again. Check answers with the class. You could write the sentence pairs on the board and show the references using arrows. Note that pair 1b contains two uses of reference: one using a personal pronoun (*she* to *Rebecca*) and one using a possessive determiner (*their* to *the Kombai people*).

Answers

1 In Papua New Guinea, <u>Rebecca</u> meets <u>the Kombai people</u>.

     ↕   ↕

b <u>She</u> tells the story of <u>their</u> traditional lifestyle.

2 a   3 d   4 c

Language note

Using pronouns and possessive determiners to refer back to preceding nouns or noun phrases (referencing) is an important cohesive device in writing. It can make a text more fluent and natural. It also avoids repetition which can make a text stilted and unnatural.

Optional activity

👥 To round off the lesson, write these questions on the board and ask learners to discuss them in pairs. For feedback, ask one or two learners to report back to the class.

Would you like to visit Papua New Guinea?
Do you like the tree houses? Would you like to live in one?
How is life in the Kombai village different from life in your town or city?

READING 2

PREPARING TO READ

Optional activity

To lead into Reading 2 about the daily routine of a university student, you could discuss the following questions with individual learners / the whole class:

How is your day/week going?
Are you busy?
Do students work too hard in your country?
Do students need more holidays?

1 👤 Focus on the wordbox and the table. Make sure learners understand the column headings, e.g. *subject* (here = an area of knowledge studied in a school, university, etc.). Contrast it with the grammatical term *subject*, which learners already know.

Elicit one or two answers from the whole class as examples. Learners complete the rest of the table using the glossary or a dictionary to help them. Check answers with the class. You could write or project the table onto the board and get learners to write in the answers there.

Answers

verb: get up, take, study, relax
adjective: busy, quiet, late, early
name of a subject: Maths, Engineering, Physics
part of the day: evening, morning, afternoon
day of the week: Tuesday, Friday, Monday, Wednesday

PREVIEWING

2 👤 Focus on the timetable and the text. Revise *timetable* if necessary. Focus on statements (1–3). Learners quickly preview the timetable and the text to decide if they are true or false. You could set a time limit of 10–15 seconds to make sure learners do this quickly. Check the answers with the class.

Answers

1 T   2 F   3 T

Language note

Notice the typical features of timetables: abbreviations for days of the week (i.e. the first three or four letters of the word, e.g. *Mon, Thurs*); and the abbreviations *am* (from Latin *ante meridiem* [= before midday]) or *pm* (from Latin *post meridiem* [= after midday]) to indicate morning or afternoon. Some learners may wish to use these abbreviations when they write a timetable for their partner in the Critical thinking section.

WHILE READING

SCANNING TO FIND INFORMATION

3 👤👥 Focus on the *Scanning* explanation box and revise scanning techniques learnt so far (e.g. looking for numbers or names as described in Unit 2) if necessary. In addition to numbers and names, learners can also scan for key words (see Language note below).

Focus on Exercise 3 and point out that the key words learners need to look for in the texts are underlined. Learners must circle the correct italicized options to complete the sentences. Demonstrate the activity by doing the first one or two together with the class. Learners circle the remaining options. To make sure that learners scan for key words rather than read closely, set a time limit of two or three minutes for this. Learners can check their answers in pairs. Check answers with the class. Ask: *What do you think of Abdullah's timetable?*

Answers

1 Thursday evening 2 Cairo 3 busy 4 three
5 cinema 6 morning 7 early 8 five
9 Thursday 10 Engineering

Language note

A key word or important word means a content word which carries information relevant to the search (usually a noun, verb or adjective). This is in contrast to function words which show grammatical relationship rather than lexical meaning (e.g. auxiliary verbs, determiners, prepositions).

DISCUSSION

4 👥 Learners ask and answer the questions in pairs. For feedback, ask one or two learners to tell the class their or their partner's answers.

⊙ LANGUAGE DEVELOPMENT

COLLOCATIONS

Optional activity

👤 You could lead into the Language development section by revising some of the new vocabulary covered in the unit so far. Write the two columns of words below on the board and ask learners to join each item on the left to one or more items on the right to make a meaningful phrase or collocation. Check answers with the class.

hunt	photographs
cook	150 kilometres
traditional	lifestyle
get up	food
travel	animals
amazing	early

Answers

hunt animals
cook food
traditional lifestyle/food
get up early
travel 150 kilometres
amazing photographs/food

1 👤 Focus on the *Collocations* explanation box. Highlight the verb + noun and verb + prepositional phrase collocations and

write them on the board. Elicit other related examples, e.g.:

meals and drinks: *have breakfast/lunch/dinner/tea/coffee*
sports: *play football/tennis*
study subjects: *study Maths/English/History*
activities: *go to the cinema/theatre/shopping centre/library/gym*

With a stronger class, you could also teach/revise phrases for everyday activities where the definite article is dropped, e.g. *go to bed/school/work.*

Elicit the first answer to Exercise 1 from the class. Learners match the remaining sentence halves. Check answers with the class.

Answers

1 b 2 c 3 e 4 a 5 d

Language note

A collocation means a word or phrase which is often used with another word or phrase, in a way that sounds correct to people who speak the language well.

2 👤 Focus on the gapped sentences. You could ask learners to read the sentences first and think about what the missing verbs could be before looking for them in the wordbox. Remind them about matching singular and plural subjects and verbs. With a stronger class, you could point out use of the Present simple for these statements of general fact/habitual actions. (This is focused on in the Grammar for writing section later in the unit.) Learners complete the exercise individually. Check answers with the class.

Answers

1 live 2 has 3 go 4 reads 5 have 6 eats/has
7 relax 8 do 9 cooks 10 go

VOCABULARY FOR STUDY

3 👥 Focus on the table. Explain the meaning of Arts and Humanities (see Language note below). Elicit the correct category for one or two of the subjects in the table as examples. Learners work in pairs to complete the table, using the glossary to help them. Check answers with the class. Discuss any subjects which the class think could go into more than one category, e.g. Geography. You could also ask learners which subjects they would like to study further.

Answers

subject	Arts and Humanities	Business	Science	Languages
Maths			✓	
Physics			✓	
Literature	✓			
English				✓
Economics		✓		
Biology			✓	
History	✓			
Management		✓		
Arabic				✓
Geography	✓			
Chemistry			✓	
Art and Design	✓			

Language note

Academic subjects are often divided into categories and taught through corresponding departments in universities and colleges. Arts and Humanities are grouped together in the table because there is some overlap in the subjects they cover. Generally, the Humanities include subjects that are concerned with human culture and ideas, e.g. Literature, History, Geography and Philosophy. Arts subjects can mean any subjects that are not Sciences or Business, but can also include Art, Design, Music and Drama.

CRITICAL THINKING

Go through the instructions with the class and focus on the writing task. Explain that the following sections of the unit will help them to prepare to write factual sentences about the lifestyle of a student in their class.

REMEMBER

1 👥 Learners could prepare for this exercise by writing down headings for the information they are going to ask for, e.g. *Name, School/University, Subjects*, etc. You may also decide to move learners away from their usual partners so that they have someone new to interview. Learners ask and answer in pairs,

noting down the information. Monitor and give support where needed.

CREATE

2 👤 Refer learners back to Abdullah's timetable on page 58. You could again highlight the use of abbreviations for days and the method for showing times. Provide a model by asking a strong learner one or two questions about his/her partner's timetable and writing a partial timetable based on his their answers on the board. Learners then complete the blank timetable with the information they noted down for their partner. Monitor and give support where needed.

WRITING

GRAMMAR FOR WRITING

Focus on the *Subject – Verb – Object* explanation box. Revise *subject* and *verb* and *explain* object. Remind learners that a prepositional phrase consists of a preposition and a noun/noun phrase (see Unit 2). As learners complete the next two exercises, ask them to use the explanation box information to help them. You could also refer to this when checking the answers as a class, particularly for problematic answers (i.e. if several students have made the same error).

Language note

Subject – Verb – Object (S – V – O) is the usual word order of an English sentence. An object is a person or thing (a noun, pronoun or noun phrase) that is affected in a direct way by the action of a verb. A what-question can ask for information about the object of a verb, e.g. *What does Li Mei have? She has lunch. What does my grandfather read? He reads a newspaper,* etc. The prepositional phrases *in the library / in Cairo* answer the question *Where?*, not *What?*, and do not give information about the object.

A noun/noun phrase/adjective after *is/are* or another form of *be* is a complement, not an object. In the sentence *Abdullah is a student, a student* = a complement. Linking verbs, such as *be*, do not have objects.

---

1 👤👥 Focus on the first sentence and ask if the bold words are an object or not (Answer: not). Elicit the reason (because they come after *are*). Learners tick the remaining sentences with objects, then check their answers in pairs. Check answers with the whole class. With some learners, it may be helpful to ask questions to reinforce the object idea here,

e.g. *What does Attila do in the morning? What do you have every morning? What does Somlek study? What does Ayşe have in the morning? What does your teacher ask?*

With stronger learners you could go through what the other non-objects are:

1 adverb + adjective after *is/are*
(= complement)
6 and 8 = prepositional phrases

Answers

The bold words and phrases in sentences 2, 3, 4, 5 and 7 are objects.

2 Focus on the jumbled sentences. Learners put the words in the correct order to make sentences. Check answers with the class. Elicit two possible versions of question 5.

Answers

1 The Kombai eat meat.
2 Kombai men hunt animals.
3 Rebecca Moore writes books.
4 Abdullah reads books in the library.
5 Melody drinks coffee in the morning. / In the morning, Melody drinks coffee.

Present simple

Focus on the *Present simple* explanation box. Elicit what learners understand by 'typical lifestyle' here (see also the Language note below). You could draw a simple timetable for your week on the board and elicit statements for your regular activities using the Present simple, e.g. *Mr Ali goes to the gym on Tuesday evenings / has dinner at 8 pm,* etc. (Keep the timetable on the board for the next activity.) Then, elicit personalized statements from learners about their own regular activities. Revise singular noun/pronoun plus singular verb as well as the spelling of the third person singular ending and the correct spellings of *goes* and *has*.

Language note

We use the Present simple to talk about the things we usually/regularly do and things that are generally true about our lives, e.g. *I like apples.* The Present simple is often contrasted with the Present continuous which is used to refer to continuous events which are happening at the present moment, e.g. *I am eating an apple.*

3 Focus on the text and elicit the first two or three answers from the class as examples.

Learners circle the remaining correct verb forms. Check answers with the class and highlight the correct spelling of *studies.*

Answers

1 is 2 is 3 studies 4 gets up 5 has
6 has 7 has 8 studies 9 goes 10 is

Time expressions

Focus on the *Time expressions* explanation box. Highlight the use of the Present simple with *every* + noun time expressions, i.e. for regular activities. Elicit further examples from learners. You could also reuse the timetable of your regular activities from the previous activity to elicit Present simple sentences using time expressions with *on* and *in* for regular activities. In addition to *at* + clock time, you could also teach the expression *at night* and contrast this with *in + the + morning/ afternoon/evening.*

Optional activity

After looking at the *Time expressions* box, ask learners to close their books. Write *at, in* and *on* on the board and elicit one example of a time expression for each preposition. Write these next to the correct prepositions, then ask learners to make a note of them.

4 Ask learners to complete the sentences without looking at the explanation box. Monitor to see how well they can complete the exercise. Then ask them to look at the explanation box to check their answers. Check answers with the class. Point out that either *on* or *every* can be used with days of the week in sentences describing regular activities.

Answers

1 on/every; at 2 In 3 On/Every; at 4 in
5 On/Every; at 6 on/every 7 in 8 at

ACADEMIC WRITING SKILLS

Spelling

Focus on the *Spelling* explanation box and introduce/revise vowels and consonants.

You could highlight the different spelling patterns of the Present simple third person singular verb forms by using coloured pens to write them on the board. Revise the different spellings learners have already encountered in the unit, e.g. *goes, has, studies*. With stronger learners, elicit other examples of each pattern, e.g. *ies: try/tries, fly/flies, marry/marries, cry/cries*; vowel + -*y*: *play/plays, stay/stays*.

Language note

Note also the spelling of verbs ending in -*s*, -*ch*, -*z*, -*sh* which also add -*es*, e.g. *miss/misses, buzz/buzzes, watch/watches, teach/teaches, push/pushes, fix/fixes*.

Optional activity

To practise vowels and consonants, ask learners to write down two headings: *vowels* and *consonants*. Read out five consonants randomly mixed with the five vowels, e.g. *o, r, e, j, a, t, h, u, i, y*. Learners write the letters in the correct columns. Check answers with the class.

---

1 👤 Learners complete the table with the correct third person singular forms. Check answers with the class.

> **Answers**
>
> gets up sells goes studies pays has

2 👥 Focus on the jumbled subject words and elicit the first answer from the class. Highlight the normal use of an initial capital letter for school/university subjects. Learners write the remaining correct subjects. You could add a competitive element by putting learners in pairs and giving them a time limit; the pair with the most correct answers when the time is up are the winners. Check answers with the class, paying particular attention to spelling.

> **Answers**
>
> 1 Maths 2 English 3 Physics 4 Engineering
> 5 History 6 Biology 7 Geography

WRITING TASK

WRITE A FIRST DRAFT

1 👤 Learners look again at the timetable they made in the Critical thinking section.

2 👤 Learners complete the gapped sentences with information about their partner.

3 👤 Learners follow the prompts to write more sentences that are true for their partners. If necessary, you can use the prompts in

Exercise 3 and the text about Abdullah on page 59 as the basis for giving more support with the writing task. Ask learners to find the corresponding information about Abdullah, e.g. *What does he study?* Write the answers on the board showing how these sentences match the prompts.

1 Write a sentence about the subject(s) he/she studies, e.g. *He studies Engineering at Cairo University.*

2 Write a sentence about the time he/she gets up, e.g. *He gets up at 6 am every day,* etc.

3 Revise *from … to …* with specific times to show duration (see also Unit 2) for sentences describing a timetable, e.g. *Abdullah has three classes every morning. He has Physics from 8 am to 9 am, Maths from 9.15 am to 10.15 am*, etc.

4 Highlight the position of prepositional phrases of time (i.e. at the beginning of the sentences) in sentences about evening and free-time activities and contrast with other sentences where these come at the end, e.g. *In the evening, Abdullah studies in the library. In his free time, Abdullah relaxes with friends and sometimes he goes to the cinema.* This is one of the points on the task checklist below.

EDIT

4 and 5 👤 Focus on the task checklist. Go through the checklist together to make sure the learners know what to check. Then ask learners to edit their sentences, using the checklist to help them. When they have checked and revised their writing, they can hand it in to you for marking. If the writing task has produced some common errors, you can look at these in the next lesson and use the model answer to highlight any particular areas.

> **Answers**
>
> See page 132 for a model answer.

Optional activity

Ask students to identify similarities and differences between their own work and the model answer and the Abdullah Taha text. Ask students to underline examples of language from the unit (e.g. time expressions, third person singular verb endings/spellings, Subject – Verb – Object word order) in both their work and the models. Give feedback by discussing these as a class.

OBJECTIVES REVIEW

See Introduction, page 9, for ideas about using the Objectives Review with your learners.

WORDLIST

See Introduction, page 9, for ideas about how to make the most of the Wordlist with your learners.

REVIEW TEST

See page 105 for the photocopiable Review Test for this unit and page 94, for ideas about when and how to administer the Review Test.

RESEARCH PROJECT

Create a lifestyle magazine.

Explain to your learners that they are going to research different elements to create a lifestyle magazine. An element is assigned to a group. They can do this in any word processing or layout program. Instruct learners to use internet poster creation sites to help them with images and design. The elements can include: health, family, entertainment, food, finances, fashion, the home, the garden, holidays and sport

Tell learners they will write, design and distribute their magazine to all the learners in their learning environment.

4 PLACES

Learning objectives

Go through the learning objectives with the class to make sure everyone understands what they can expect to achieve in this unit. Point out that learners will have a chance to review these objectives again at the end of the unit.

UNLOCK YOUR KNOWLEDGE

Lead-in

👥 Play a matching game. Write the two columns below on the board. (Take this opportunity to pre-teach *capital* and *country*.) In pairs, learners match the capitals to the correct countries. Ask pairs to raise their hands as soon as they have finished. The first pair to match correctly are the winners.

country /ˈkʌntri/	capital /ˈkæpɪtl/
France	Ottawa
Morocco	Jakarta
Turkey	Tokyo
Indonesia	Canberra
India	Rabat
Japan	Paris
China	New Delhi
Canada	Beijing
Australia	Ankara

Answers

France, Paris Morocco, Rabat Turkey, Ankara
Indonesia, Jakarta India, New Delhi Japan, Tokyo
China, Beijing Canada, Ottawa Australia, Canberra

1 👥 Focus on the photograph of the Grand Canyon and ask: *Do you know this famous place? Where is it?* Focus on the lists of famous places and cities. Learners match the famous places to the correct cities. Check answers with the class. Ask: *Have you visited any of these places? What did you think of it/ them? Did you like it? What did you do there?*

Answers

1 The Louvre-d Paris
2 The Sphinx-f Giza
3 Taipei 101-e Taipei
4 Palm Island-b Dubai
5 The Golden Gate Bridge-c San Francisco
6 The Blue Mosque-a Istanbul

Background note

The Grand Canyon is a deep canyon made by the Colorado River in Arizona in the USA. It is 277 miles long and up to 18 miles wide.

The Louvre in Paris, France, is one of the largest museums and art galleries in the world. (See video still on Student's Book page 70.)

Taipei 101 in Taipei, the capital of Taiwan, was the world's tallest building from 2004 to 2011, with a height of 509 metres (1,670 feet). (See also Student's Book, page 129.)

The Golden Gate Bridge spans San Francisco Bay, California, USA.

The Sphinx in Giza is an ancient Egyptian statue of a mythical creature with a lion's body and a human head.

The Palm Islands in Dubai, United Arab Emirates, are man-made islands created for residential, leisure and entertainment use.

The seventeenth-century Blue Mosque, also called the Sultan Ahmet Mosque, is in Istanbul, Turkey. It is famous for the blue tiles on its interior walls.

2 👥 Learners ask and answer the questions in pairs. For feedback, ask one or two pairs to report back to the class.

WATCH AND LISTEN

Optional activity

Focus on the video stills at the top of the page and ask learners to say what they can see. Use the pictures to pre-teach *mountains* and *race*.

PREPARING TO WATCH

UNDERSTANDING KEY VOCABULARY

1 👤 Focus on the wordbox and the gapped sentences. Learners complete the sentences with the words in the box. Check answers with the class and model and drill pronunciation of any difficult words, e.g. *tourist* /ˈtʊərɪst/, *mountain* /ˈmaʊntɪn/ and *tower* /taʊə/.

Answers

1 Tourists 2 races 3 cheese 4 mountains
5 capital city 6 tower

Background note

Mount Fuji is the highest mountain in Japan at 3,776 metres (12,389 feet).

Jebel Hafeet is the highest named mountain in the United Arab Emirates. It is mostly in the UAE, partly in Oman and is 1,249 metres high (4,097 feet).

Ağrı Dağı, also known in English as Mount Ararat, is the highest mountain in Turkey at 5,137 metres (16,854 feet).

Kilimanjaro is the highest mountain in Kenya and also the highest in Africa at 5,895 metres (19,341 feet).

USING YOUR KNOWLEDGE TO PREDICT CONTENT

2 Tell learners that they are going to prepare for watching a video about France by doing a quiz about the country. This should help them activate their existing knowledge. Elicit or pre-teach the meaning of *quiz* /kwɪz/ and use the images in the book to teach *flag*. (Learners check their answers when they watch in the next exercise.)

WHILE WATCHING

UNDERSTANDING MAIN IDEAS

3 Play the video so that learners can check their answers to the quiz in Exercise 2. After viewing, let them discuss their answers in pairs. Check answers with the class. Ask if any learners have ever visited France.

Answers

1 b 2 c 3 b 4 c 5 a

LISTENING FOR KEY INFORMATION

4 Go through the numbers in the box, eliciting, modelling and drilling the pronunciation.

3 three
20 twenty
350 three hundred and fifty
450 four hundred and fifty

3,000 three thousand
30,000 thirty thousand
60,000 sixty thousand
6,000,000 six million
35,000,000 thirty-five million

Play the video again. Learners watch and circle the numbers they hear.

Answers

3 6,000,000 30,000 20 350

Language note

Notice the use of *and* in *three hundred and fifty* and *four hundred and fifty*; *and* is only used after hundreds and before tens.

5 Focus on the gapped sentences. Elicit/explain the meaning of *work of art* in question 3 (plural: *works of art* = something an artist makes, especially a painting, drawing or statue). Elicit the first correct number to complete question 1. Learners complete the remaining sentences with the correct numbers from Exercise 4. Check answers with the class. Ask: *Are you surprised by any of these facts? Do you know the names of any French cheeses?* (e.g. Brie, Camembert)

Answers

1 3 2 6,000,000 3 30,000 4 20 5 350

Video script

France is in Western Europe. It is famous for its culture, fine food and beautiful countryside.

The French flag is called the Tricolore. It is red, white and blue.

Paris is the capital city of France. Paris is an important city for business and tourism.

This is the Eiffel Tower. It is the most famous place in Paris. Six million tourists visit the tower every year. Another famous place is The Louvre. There are 30,000 works of art in this museum!

Tourists enjoy the fine food. There are 20 different kinds of bread and 350 different kinds of cheese in France. The food comes from the many farms in France.

France is also famous for its mountains, the Alps and Pyrenees. The Tour de France bicycle race happens every year. The cyclists race all over France.

France is an interesting place to visit.

DISCUSSION

6 👥 Focus on the questions. Learners ask and answer in pairs. Monitor and make a note of interesting information they find out, e.g. unusual foods. Conduct full class feedback and ask a few pairs to tell the class what they have found out. Encourage able learners to use more complex language, e.g. *(capital city) is the capital of (country). Lots of tourists visit (capital city) especially in the (summer). They usually visit (list of famous places). Lots of different kinds of food are popular in (country). Many people have (food items) for breakfast and (food items) for lunch. For dinner, people like to eat (food items). There are some / aren't any mountains in (country). They are called (name of mountain/mountain range).*

Optional activity

👥 Put learners in pairs and ask them to write multiple-choice quiz questions like those in Exercise 2 about their country for another pair to answer. They can use photographs from the Internet to illustrate their quiz.

READING 1

PREPARING TO READ

UNDERSTANDING KEY VOCABULARY

1 👤 Ask learners to match the words (1–7) to their definitions (a–g). Check answers with the class. Model and drill pronunciation of *ancient* /ˈeɪntʃənt/.

Answers
1 g 2 e 3 a 4 c 5 f 6 b 7 d

2 👤 Focus on the wordbox and the gapped sentences. Learners complete the sentences using the glossary on page 196 to help them. Check answers with the class. Model and drill pronunciation of *forest* /ˈfɒrɪst/ and *ocean* /ˈəʊʃn/.

Answers
1 Lake 2 Sea 3 mountains 4 forest 5 rivers
6 Ocean

PREVIEWING

3 👤 Briefly remind learners about the previewing they have already done in previous units. Focus on the multiple-choice questions.

Learners glance at the text and the picture and circle the correct answers. Again, you could set a short time limit of 10–15 seconds for this to ensure learners preview quickly. Check answers with the class.

Answers
1 c 2 b 3 b

WHILE READING

Background note

The extracts here are from a popular history book. The contents page, a map and part of a chapter are shown on a webpage from a bookseller's website.

SCANNING TO FIND INFORMATION

4 👤 Focus on the listed items and the table of contents. Point out that some of the chapters are numbered 1, 2, etc. and some have subsections numbered 2.1 (two point one), 3.1, etc. Revise scanning techniques from previous units, i.e. remind learners to look for key words and capital letters in names. Point out that learners should also look for related words, e.g. *Greek* for *Greece*, *Roman* for *Rome*, and make educated guesses where necessary, as not all the chapter titles are exactly the same as the list items. Elicit the first answer as an example. Learners match the remaining items to the correct chapters of the book. Check answers with the class.

Answers
1 Chapter 3.3 2 Chapter 2.1 3 Chapter 4.1
4 Chapter 6 5 Chapter 2.2

Background note

The Chinese minister, geographer and cartographer Pei Xiu (224–271) worked in the Chinese state of Cao Wei during the Three Kingdoms period.

Ancient Greece refers to the period of Greek civilization that began in the eighth century BC and lasted until the sixth century AD.

The Persian mathematician, astronomer and geographer Al-Khwarizmi (780–850) worked in Baghdad during the Abbasid Empire.

Ancient Rome refers to the period of Roman civilization that includes the Roman Republic, the Roman Empire and the Western Roman Empire. It began in the eighth century BC and lasted until the fourth century BC approximately.

5 👤 Focus on the table and elicit/explain the difference between *continent* (= a very large area of land which is usually divided into countries) and *country*. Learners scan both texts and circle the continents/countries that are mentioned in them. Check answers with the class and drill pronunciation of any difficult words.

> **Answers**
>
> continents: Asia /ˈeɪʒə/, Europe /ˈjʊərəp/, America /əˈmerɪkə/, Africa /ˈæfrɪkə/
> countries: Spain /speɪn/, Norway /ˈnɔːweɪ/, China /ˈtʃaɪnə/

READING FOR DETAIL

6 👤 Focus on Figure 4.3. Ask learners if they notice anything unusual about the map. (Elicit or point out that north is at the bottom of the map and south is at the top.) Ask learners if they can recognize any continents or countries. (It will help them to turn their books round.) Ask: *Can you find Africa/Europe/the Mediterranean Sea/the Arabian peninsula/Asia?*

Focus on the statements. Learners read the extract and mark each statement as T or F. Check answers with the class and elicit the correct versions of the false statements. Ask: *Why isn't America on the map?* (Because it hadn't been discovered by people from Europe/Africa when Muhammad al-Idrisi made the map.)

> **Answers**
>
> 1 F He was Moroccan / from Morocco.
> 2 F It is the Latin name of the map.
> 3 T
> 4 T
> 5 T

> **Background note**
>
> Muhammad al-Idrisi was a geographer, cartographer and traveller. Born in Ceuta, Morocco, he travelled through North Africa, Anatolia and many parts of Europe before moving to Sicily to work for the Norman king, Roger II. Here he drew the Tabula Rogeriana in 1154, a very accurate map for its time.

> **Optional activity**
>
> 👥 To round off the lesson, write these questions on the board and ask learners to discuss them in pairs. Ask one or two learners to report back to the class.

> Can you read a map?
> Is it important to know how to read a map?
> Is Satnav better? Why? (Satnav = satellite navigation)
> When did you last use a map?

READING 2

PREPARING TO READ

UNDERSTANDING KEY VOCABULARY

1 👤👥 Focus on the first group of words and elicit the word that is different from the rest (*France*). You could ask learners why it is different. Learners circle the other different words, then check their answers in pairs. Check answers with the class. Ask stronger learners to give reasons for their choices if possible.

> **Answers**
>
> 1 France (The other words describe areas of water.)
> 2 road (The other words are buildings.)
> 3 ocean (The other words are man-made places.)
> 4 drive (The other words describe activities in water.)

2 👤 Learners match words to their definitions. Check answers with the class and highlight the spelling and pronunciation of *currency* /ˈkʌrənsi/, *population* /ˌpɒpjʊˈleɪʃən/, *tourism* /ˈtʊərɪzəm/, and *delicious* /dɪˈlɪʃəs/. Elicit sentences using these words from learners to personalize them.

> **Answers**
>
> 1 b 2 c 3 d 4 a

PREVIEWING

3 👤 Focus on the statements and possible options. Check learners understand *popular* /ˈpɒpjʊlə/ (= liked or enjoyed by many people). Learners preview the text and circle the correct options. Check answers with the class. You could elicit the headings/paragraphs where learners found the relevant information here.

> **Answers**
>
> 1 c 2 b 3 c

WHILE READING

READING FOR MAIN IDEAS

4 👤 Focus on the *Reading for main ideas* explanation box, making sure learners understand what a paragraph is. Highlight the topic and important information in the example sentence.

Focus on the topics (1–8). Make sure learners understand the topics and elicit the kinds of information they would expect to find in the relevant paragraphs of the text, e.g. names of languages and words like *speak* for languages, numbers of people for population, jobs and/or businesses for the economy, etc. Elicit the first answer as an example. Learners match the remaining topics to the correct paragraphs (A–H). Check answers with the class. Check understanding and model and drill pronunciation of the words in the Fact File, e.g. *religion* /rɪˈlɪdʒən/, *climate* /ˈklaɪmət/ (elicit another word, e.g. *weather*) and *industry* /ˈɪndəstri/.

> **Answers**
> 1 D 2 B 3 F 4 E 5 H 6 A 7 G 8 C

DISCUSSION

5 👥 Learners ask and answer the questions in pairs. For feedback, ask one or two learners to tell the class their or their partner's answers.

> **Optional activity**
>
> If possible, extend the discussion by allowing learners time to research their answers on the Internet and make a note of the information before they ask and answer. Help out with vocabulary as required, e.g. words for businesses and industries.

⊙ LANGUAGE DEVELOPMENT

VOCABULARY FOR PLACES IN A CITY

1 👤👥 Focus on the picture and the wordbox. Elicit the correct place on the picture for the first word as an example. Learners label the picture with the remaining words from the box. Advise them to use a pencil rather than a pen for this. Learners check answers with a partner. Check answers with the class and check pronunciation by modelling and drilling any difficult words as necessary, e.g. *museum* /mjuːˈziːəm/, *university* /ˌjuːnɪˈvɜːsɪti/, *monument* /ˈmɒnjʊmənt/, *factory* /ˈfæktəri/, *library* /ˈlaɪbrəri/, *fountain* /ˈfaʊntɪn/. Elicit sentences using the new words: *Is there a museum/park/monument in your city? Where is the library?* etc.

> **Answers**
> factory
> train station
> bank
> bridge
> monument
> library
> university
> museum
> park
> fountain

> **Language note**
>
> Point out that *a* is used before *university* (not *an*) because it has a /j/ sound at the beginning. The use of *a* or *an* depends on the pronunciation of the first letter at the start of a word.

Noun phrases with *of*

2 👤 Focus on the *Noun phrases* explanation box and highlight the pattern: noun + *of* + a noun. Focus on the sentence halves and elicit the first answer. Learners match the sentence halves. Check answers with the class.

> **Answers**
> 1 d 2 e 3 a 4 c 5 b

> **Language note**
>
> These noun + *of* + a noun phrases are usually used with inanimate things. Possessive *'s* is used with people or when talking about time, e.g. *Jane's hat, next year's prices*. We say/write *the capital of France, the centre of the country* (not *France's capital, the country's centre*).

VOCABULARY FOR PLACES IN A COUNTRY

1 👤 👥 Focus on the picture and the wordbox. Learners label the picture with the words from the box. Advise them to use a pencil rather than a pen for this. Learners check answers with a partner. Check answers with the class and check pronunciation by modelling and drilling any difficult words as necessary, e.g. *field* /fiːld/, *forest* /ˈfɒrɪst/, *valley* /ˈvæli/ and *beach* /biːtʃ/.

> **Answers**
> sea
> mountains
> desert
> hill
> forest
> farm
> valley
> field
> beach
> cliff

CRITICAL THINKING

Go through the instructions with the class and focus on the writing task. Explain that the following sections of the unit will help them to prepare to write facts about their country.

CREATE

Focus on the *Planning* box. Explain that when we plan our writing, we think about putting our ideas in a logical order, i.e. in order of importance.

1 👤 👥 Focus on the wordbox and explain that these topics are often included in a factual description of a country. Remind learners that they are preparing to write about their country and ask them to list the topics in a logical order in column A of the table. Learners can look at the Fact File on the Maldives to help with this, but they do not have to follow the order given there. Learners compare their answers and discuss them. Elicit some suggested orders from individual learners and discuss them with the whole class. A suggested order is given below, but alternatives are possible, particularly with the last few categories. Accept any order that is logical.

> **Answers**
> full name, population, capital city, geography, climate, language, religion, currency, industry, food

APPLY

Focus on the *Classifying* box. Explain that classifying means grouping words according to their relevance to different topics.

2 👤 Here learners think of key words linked to each topic and make a note of them in the table. Demonstrate by completing an example on the board with the whole class, e.g. *For language in the Maldives, we could write: speak: Dhivehi; English: useful, tourists.* Learners write the key words for each topic in column B of the table; they could research some of the key words using the Internet. Encourage learners to use their dictionaries. Monitor and help as required. This task will provide learners with clearly structured notes for the Writing task.

> **Answers**
> Answers will vary.

WRITING

GRAMMAR FOR WRITING

Focus on the *there is / there are* explanation box. Ask learners to read it and encourage an able learner to summarize the explanation, i.e. Use *there is* before singular nouns and *there are* before plural nouns.

> **Language note**
>
> We use *There is/are* when we talk/write about a new topic for the first time and we want to introduce it. We also use *There is/are* to show that something is or exists, e.g. *There is an airport in Malé.* (not *An airport is in Malé.*)

> **Optional activity**
>
> Practise *there is/are* by saying a noun and asking learners to put it in a sentence with the correct form, *there is* or *there are*. For example: *an airport in Malé = There is an airport in Malé. 350 different kinds of cheese in France = There are 350 different kinds of cheese in France.*

1 👤👥 Focus on the jumbled words and elicit the first correct sentence as an example. Learners put the remaining words in order to make sentences, then check in pairs. Check answers with the class. Check understanding of *palace* /'pælɪs/ in sentence 5.

> **Answers**
>
> 1 There are different kinds of business in my country.
> 2 There are 36 languages in Senegal.
> 3 There are three modern airports in my city.
> 4 There is a big museum of art in Seoul.
> 5 There is a famous palace in my city.

2 👤 Ask learners to read the sentences and put a tick if they are correct or a cross if they are wrong. Elicit the first answer from the class. Learners work individually. Check answers with the class.

> **Answers**
>
> correct: 1, 4, 7
> wrong: 2, 3, 5, 6, 8

3 👤 Ask learners to correct the wrong sentences from Exercise 2. Demonstrate the activity by correcting sentence 1 together on the board. Learners correct the remaining wrong sentences. Check answers with the class. Point out that number 6 has incorrect word order rather than incorrect words and revise the position of prepositional phrases.

> **Answers**
>
> 2 There are deserts in Egypt. / There is a desert in Egypt.
> 3 There are many parks in London.
> 5 There are many people in Jakarta.
> 6 There are many bridges in Istanbul.
> 8 There is a famous museum in my city.

Determiners: articles

Focus on the *Determiners: articles* box and the different categories which have the article *the* in front of them and those which have no article *the*. You could elicit some local examples of rivers, seas, countries, cities, etc. to personalize the language and make it relevant to your learners. Write other seas, oceans, famous places, groups of islands, continents, cities, etc. on the board and ask learners to say whether they have articles or not.

4 👤 Focus on the gapped sentences and explain the instructions. Elicit the first answer as an example. Check answers with the class.

> **Answers**
>
> 1 0 2 0; 0 3 the 4 The 5 the 6 0

5 👤 This time ask learners not to look at the *Determiners* explanation box while they complete the exercise. Tell them to look at the box to check their answers. Check answers with the class using the board.

> **Answers**
>
> 1 I come from the India.
> 2 The Paris is popular with tourists.
> 3 There are many tall buildings in the Abu Dhabi.
> 4 There are 3 million people in the Nagoya in the Japan.
> 5 The United Kingdom is in the Europe.
> 6 Many people live in the Cairo.
> 7 The Ural mountains are in the Russia.

ACADEMIC WRITING SKILLS
SPELLING

Capital letters

1 👤 Go through the *Capital letters* box. Focus on the table and complete the first nationality adjective on the board with the class. Learners complete the other adjectives individually, using their dictionaries to help. Check answers with the class, writing or projecting the table onto the board and getting individual learners to fill it in.

> **Answers**
>
> | country | nationality |
> | --- | --- |
> | China | Chinese |
> | India | Indian |
> | Egypt | Egyptian |
> | Saudi Arabia | Saudi |
> | The United Arab Emirates | Emirati |
> | Algeria | Algerian |
> | Japan | Japanese |
> | Thailand | Thai |
> | Turkey | Turkish |
> | France | French |
> | The United Kingdom | British |
> | Canada | Canadian |
> | Chile | Chilean |

Language note

Notice some of the common nationality adjective endings: -ish for *English, Spanish*; -an for *Moroccan, German*; -ian for *Algerian, Indian, Egyptian*; -ean for *Chilean, Korean*; -ese for *Chinese, Japanese* and -i for *Saudi, Emerati, Thai.*

2 🏃 Focus on the sentences. Correct the first sentence on the board with the class. Revise the use of a capital letter for the first letter of the first word in a sentence and a full stop at the end. Learners correct the remaining sentences. Check answers with the class.

Answers

1 I come from Abu Dhabi.
2 There are many beautiful fountains in Rome.
3 The climate is good in the Maldives.
4 There are four main islands in Japan.
5 Chicken is very popular in Malaysia.

WRITING TASK

WRITE A FIRST DRAFT

1 and 2 🏃 Refer learners back to the table of topics and key words they completed in the Critical thinking section. Then focus on the example sentences about Thailand. Ask learners to write two sentences for each topic about their country, using the key words they added to the table. If your class would benefit from this, you could do a further example together on the board. Learners could also look at the text about the Maldives on page 77 for ideas. Monitor and help as necessary.

EDIT

3 and 4 🏃 Focus on the task checklist. Go through the checklist to make sure learners know what to check. Then ask learners to edit their work, using the checklist to help them. You can ask learners to produce a final draft of their work before handing it in. If not, collect in their edited first draft to mark and correct. If the writing task has produced some common errors, highlight these in later lessons, using the model answer to give examples. Choose some good examples of writing from individual

learners and ask them if you can share them with the class. These could be displayed on the walls of the classroom, projected onto the board or photocopied and given out.

Answers

See page 133 for a model answer.

Optional activity

Ask learners to identify similarities and differences between their own work and the model answer or the Maldives text. Ask learners to underline one type of language from the unit (e.g. use of *the*/zero article with names of places, *there is/are*, or capital letters for cities, countries and adjectives for nationalities) in both their work and the models.

OBJECTIVES REVIEW

See Introduction, page 9, for ideas about using the Objectives Review with your learners.

WORDLIST

See Introduction, page 9, for ideas about how to make the most of the Wordlist with your learners.

REVIEW TEST

See page 108 for the photocopiable Review Test for this unit and page 94, for ideas about when and how to administer the Review Test.

RESEARCH PROJECT

Create a popular travel review blog.

Ask your class which places they have visited on holiday. They can be either national or international destinations. Working in pairs or groups learners will have to write an entry for a travel review blog. They will make their own blog as a class and they can comment on and rate places to eat and stay, upload photos, write about the climate, nearby nature spots, beaches, parks, and entertainment. Tell them that they will also have to think about making the blog popular with their peer group. Use the Cambridge Online creative tools to develop a class blog or decide on an alternative internet blog site that the class prefers.

5 SPORT

Learning objectives

Go through the learning objectives with the class to make sure everyone understands what they can expect to achieve in this unit. Point out that learners will have a chance to review these objectives again at the end of the unit.

UNLOCK YOUR KNOWLEDGE

Lead-in

Ask: *How many sports do you know in English?* Give learners one minute to write down as many sports in English as they can. Find out who has the most correct words and award them one point for every correct sport. Give an extra point to whoever has a sport that no one else has. Possible sports words: *football, cricket, tennis, rugby, basketball, baseball, badminton, hockey, motor racing, athletics, cycling, skating, skiing, volleyball* (plus other words from the unit and in dictionaries).

Focus on the wordbox and the table and check learners understand the headings. Model the pronunciation of *martial art* /ˈmɑːʃəl ɑːt/ (= a traditional Japanese or Chinese sport that is a type of fighting or defending yourself). Elicit the correct section of the table for *football*. Learners write the remaining sports words in the correct columns of the table. Check answers with the class.

Answers

martial art: judo, football
ball or team game: tennis, karate

WATCH AND LISTEN

Optional activity

Focus on the video stills at the top of the page and ask learners to say what they can see. Some learners may recognize Tai-chi and Kung-fu.

PREPARING TO WATCH

USING VISUALS TO PREDICT CONTENT

1 ▶ Focus on the words in the wordbox and check learners understand them. Explain the meaning of *pensioner* /ˈpenʃənə/. Play the video. Learners watch and circle the things they see. Check answers with the class.

Answers

a busy city, pensioners, morning, a teacher, young men in traditional clothes, an ancient painting

UNDERSTANDING KEY VOCABULARY

2 Elicit/check understanding of the meaning of *opposite* and elicit examples if possible. Focus on the two lists of words; you may need to give some help with the first pair. Learners match the remaining words, using a dictionary if necessary. Check answers with the class. Personalize the words by eliciting sentences which use the new vocabulary.

Answers

1 d 2 c 3 e 4 f 5 b 6 a

WHILE WATCHING

UNDERSTANDING MAIN IDEAS

3 ▶ Focus on the two questions and multiple-choice answers. Check understanding and pronunciation of *health* /helθ/, *Tai-chi* /ˌtaɪˈtʃiː/, *Kung-fu* /ˌkʌŋˈfuː/ and *culture* /ˈkʌltʃə/. Revise the meaning of *popular*. Play the video again. Learners watch and circle the correct answers. After viewing, allow them to discuss their answers in pairs. Check answers with the class. Ask: *Do you do Tai-chi or Kung-fu? What do you think of Tai-chi/Kung-fu? Would you like to do them?*

Answers

1 b 2 c

Background note

China, officially the People's Republic of China, is an Asian country stretching from Central Asia to the Pacific Ocean. It has a population of approximately 1.35 billion. It has an area of 9.6 million square kilometres (3.7 million square miles) and it is the second-largest country by land area. China has a long history reaching back nearly 4,000 years and many important things originally came from China, including paper, gunpowder, the compass, credit banking and paper money.

Video script

Life is busy in China. The people work hard. Health is important so sports and exercise are popular here. One popular kind of exercise is Tai-chi.

Every morning, about 200 million people in China do Tai-chi. It is popular with women and men. Tai-chi is a good kind of exercise for old people. It is good for the body and for the mind. It is healthy and relaxing. Tai-chi is from China. It is hundreds of years old. Tai-chi is a 'soft' martial art. That means it is slow and calm.

There are also 'hard' martial arts. These men are doing Shaolin Kung-fu. Shaolin Kung-fu is over 1,500 years old. Shaolin Kung-fu is fast and dangerous. You have to be very fit and strong to do 'hard' martial arts. The man in the brown clothes is Master Li-Yu. He teaches Shaolin Kung-fu to 30 young students. The students practise every day. They work hard. The students are young.

Li-Yu: Kung-fu is difficult. You must practise every move many times.

Sports like football and basketball are also popular in China. But martial arts like Tai-chi and Kung-fu are part of Chinese culture and history.

UNDERSTANDING DETAIL

4 ▶ 👤 Focus on the diagram and make sure learners understand the information in it, e.g. elicit the meanings of the labels with the male/female symbols (= popular with men/women). Learners complete the gaps with some (but not all) of the words from Exercise 2. Before playing the video again, you could ask learners to suggest words from Exercise 2 to fill the gaps, then they can check these guesses when they watch. Check answers with the class and if necessary be prepared to play the video more than once.

> **Answers**
> 1 slow 2 body/mind 3 mind/body 4 fast 5 strong

MAKING INFERENCES

5 👤 👥 Focus on the descriptions of four different people and their lifestyles and the different sports. Elicit the meaning of *healthy*. Explain that learners have to decide which sport or sports would suit each person best. Discuss the first answer with the whole class; more than one sport might be suitable and learners will probably have different opinions here. Learners match the remaining people and sports. Pairs discuss their answers. Check answers with the class and discuss them. Ask learners to give reasons for their answers.

> **Answers**
> 1 b or d 2 c or d 3 b 4 a

DISCUSSION

6 Focus on the questions. Students discuss them in pairs. Elicit feedback from one or two pairs at the end and broaden out the discussion to the whole class.

READING 1

PREPARING TO READ

UNDERSTANDING KEY VOCABULARY

1 👤 Focus on the words. Ask learners to match the words to their opposites. Check answers with the class and model and drill pronunciation of any difficult words, e.g. *national* /ˈnæʃənəl/, *exciting* /ɪkˈsaɪtɪŋ/, *dangerous* /ˈdeɪndʒərəs/, *local* /ˈləʊkl/ and *boring* /ˈbɔːrɪŋ/.

> **Answers**
> 1 b 2 a 3 c

2 👥 Focus on the wordbox and the gapped sentences. Learners complete the sentences, using a dictionary if necessary. Check answers with the class and model and drill pronunciation of any difficult words, e.g. *competition* /ˌkɒmpəˈtɪʃən/, *questionnaire* /ˌkwestʃəˈneə/ and *player* /ˈpleɪə/. Elicit sentences using the new words from learners to personalize the vocabulary.

Answers

1 billion 2 player 3 questionnaire 4 competitions
5 fan 6 million 7 result

USING YOUR KNOWLEDGE TO PREDICT CONTENT

Focus on the *Using your knowledge* box. Explain that asking ourselves questions before we read a text can help us read effectively because the questions give us a reason to read and also put any new information into a context.

3 🧍 Focus on the question and check understanding of *top five* (= the sports that came first, second, third, fourth and fifth in a survey of people's favourite sports). Elicit just one or two suggestions from the class at this point. Make sure learners think about the whole world here, not just the top five in their own country. Learners write their ideas.

Answers

Answers will vary.

4 👥 Learners compare their answers to Exercise 3 with a partner. Ask one or two pairs to tell the class about their lists and see whether the rest of the class agree. You could come to a class consensus on the top five and write this on the board so that learners can compare it with the reading text.

WHILE READING

READING FOR MAIN IDEAS

5 🧍 Focus learners on the sports in the box and the text. Ask them to read the text and write the correct sports above the correct paragraphs. Discuss the type of reading learners do here, i.e. they don't need to read the text very carefully, just scan quickly through each paragraph looking for words and information which are relevant to the main ideas. Remind them to look for the actual sports words in the text, but tell them that they also need to look for related words (e.g. World Cup) or the names of famous people in the sport (as the paragraphs on cricket, tennis and motor racing do not actually include the relevant sports words). (You may need to allow more time for this scanning exercise as a result.) Check answers with the class. Check understanding

and model and drill pronunciation of *cricket* /ˈkrɪkɪt/ and *hockey* /ˈhɒki/. Elicit the meaning of *motor racing*. Learners may also know another type of hockey (*ice hockey*). Compare the class consensus (above) with the top five in the text. Ask: *Are you surprised about any of the sports in the text?*

Answers

A football B cricket C field hockey D tennis
E motor racing

SCANNING TO FIND INFORMATION

6 🧍👥 Focus on the first statement and ask which paragraph learners think they will need to scan to find the answer (= B). Ask learners to scan paragraph B and elicit the answer from the class. Learners scan the magazine article again to find the answers and mark the remaining statements true or false, then check their answers in pairs. Check answers with the whole class. You could ask fast finishers to write correct versions of the false statements.

Answers

1 F Brazil has a popular football team.
2 T
3 F Ayrton Senna was from Brazil.
4 F There are 3.5 billion football fans in the world.
5 T
6 F 150 million watch Formula 1.
7 T
8 F Field hockey is the number 3 sport in the world.

Optional activity

You could encourage learners to scan the text quickly by turning the whole exercise (or one question at a time) into a race. Ask learners to close their books when they have found the answer(s). Make a note of the first three or four finishers, then check answers to see who was the first finisher with the correct answer(s).

DISCUSSION

7 👥 Learners discuss the questions in pairs. Ask one or two learners to report back to the class.

Optional activity

👥👥 If your learners are all the same nationality, ask groups to write a list of sports for their country for question 2. Ask one or two groups to tell the class about their lists and see whether the other groups agree. Come to a class consensus on the five most popular sports in their country and write this on the board.

READING 2

PREPARING TO READ

SCANNING TO PREDICT CONTENT

1 Elicit *capital letter* from learners by writing some examples on the board. Ask learners to choose the three correct answers to complete the sentence in Exercise 1. Check answers with the class.

> **Answers**
> b, c, e

2 Focus on the instructions and remind learners of scanning techniques. Ask: *What can we look for to find names?* (capital letters). To encourage quick scanning, ask learners to close their books as soon as they have found the six names.

> **Answers**
> Pelé, Kaká, Ronaldinho, Piquet, Senna, Massa

3 Ask: *Do you know these sportsmen? What do you know about them? Which sports are they famous for?* Learners talk in pairs. Conduct full class feedback.

> **Answers**
> Answers will vary.

> **Background note**
> Pelé (born 1940) is a retired footballer who scored 77 goals for the Brazil national team, making him the top scorer. He is considered by many as the best player of all time.
> Kaká (born 1982) is an attacking midfielder who has played for clubs in Brazil, France, Spain and Italy. He also plays for the Brazil national team.
> Ronaldinho (born 1980) is an attacking midfielder or forward who has played for clubs in Brazil, Italy and Spain. He also plays for the Brazil national team.
> Nelson Piquet (born 1952) is a retired racing driver who won three world championships. He is thought by many to be one of the greatest Formula 1 drivers.
> Ayrton Senna (1960–1994) was a racing driver who won three Formula 1 world championships. He was killed in an accident during the 1994 San Marino Grand Prix.
> Felipe Massa (born 1981) is a racing driver who started his Formula 1 career with Ferrari in 2003 as a test driver.

UNDERSTANDING KEY VOCABULARY

4 Focus on the words and their meanings. Elicit the first answer from the class. Learners match the remaining words, and meanings. Check answers with the class and model and drill any difficult pronunciation, e.g. *total* /'təʊtl/ and *online* /'ɒnlaɪn/. Ask questions to check understanding: *Is there a tourist office near here / in …? Do you do things online? What? Do you use the Internet a lot? How often?*

> **Answers**
> 1 d 2 a 3 e 4 b 5 f 6 c

WHILE READING

READING FOR DETAIL

> **Background note**
> The reading text comes from a guidebook about Brazil. Brazil, officially the Federative Republic of Brazil, is the largest country in South America. It is the world's fifth largest country by area (8.55 million square kilometres / 3.3 million square miles) and by population, with approximately 196.6 million people. The capital city is Brasilia, the largest city is Sao Paulo and the main language is Portuguese.

5 Focus on the statements. Learners must decide if each statement is about football, capoeira or motor racing. Give the pronunciation of *capoeira* /ˌkæpʊ'eɪrə/ and ask: *Do you know what capoeira is?* If you have Internet access, you could show learners a short video about capoeira. Elicit the first answer as an example. Remind learners that they should be reading closely this time. Learners read and complete the exercise, then check their answers in pairs. Check answers with the class.

> **Answers**
> 1 F 2 C 3 MR 4 C 5 F

6 Ask learners to read the whole gapped summary and think about which words from the reading text are missing. Elicit the first missing word from the whole class and discuss any alternative learners can think of. Learners complete the text. Check answers with the class. There is more than one possible answer

in some cases so you could discuss these alternatives with the class.

> **Answers**
>
> 1 popular / important 2 players 3 capoeira 4 park / street 5 Motor racing / Formula 1 Grand Prix 6 drivers

DISCUSSION

7 👥 Go through the list of activities for question 2 to check that learners understand them. If possible, allow learners a little time to prepare and think of reasons why each activity is/isn't a good way to exercise. Provide some model language for this, e.g. *Horse riding is a good way to exercise because you do it outside / in the fresh air. Doing housework isn't a good way to exercise because it's boring.* Learners discuss in pairs. (You could ask learners to swap pairs halfway through to vary the discussion.) For feedback, ask one or two pairs to report their opinions to the class.

⊙ LANGUAGE DEVELOPMENT

Sports collocations

Revise the meaning of *collocation* (= a word or phrase that is often used with another word or phrase, e.g. *do + homework*). Go through the *Sports collocations* explanation box with the class.

> **Optional activity**
>
> Draw the table below on the board, elicit other sports/activity words from the class, e.g. *Kung-fu, football, skiing, yoga, swimming, volleyball*, then ask individual learners to write each word in the correct column of the table.
>
> | do | play | go |
> |---|---|---|
> | Kung-fu | football | skiing |
> | yoga | volleyball | swimming |

1 👤 Focus on the wordbox, sentences (1–10) and the completed example. Learners complete the remaining sentences with the correct verbs. Encourage them to use the glossary on page 197 to help them understand the words

in bold. Check answers with the class. Ask: *Do you do any of these sports/activities? Which do you like?*

> **Answers**
>
> 1 play 2 go 3 plays 4 plays 5 play 6 do 7 play 8 goes 9 goes/go

Prepositions

Focus on the *Prepositions* explanation box and help learners notice the common collocations with *in* and *on* in these phrases. Emphasize that we use certain prepositions with particular nouns, e.g. *on television, on a farm*, and that these collocations should just be learned.

2 👥 Focus on the sentences. Elicit the first answer as an example. Learners complete the sentences with the correct prepositions, then check their answers in pairs. Check answers with the class.

> **Answers**
>
> 1 in 2 on 3 on 4 in 5 in 6 on

3 👤 Focus on the table and the bold nouns in Exercise 2. Elicit the correct column of the table for *Australia* as an example. Learners complete the table. Check answers with the class.

> **Answers**
>
> on: field, television, farm
> in: Australia, stadium, the street

Adjectives

Quickly revise adjectives by eliciting some examples. You could also write a sentence on the board and ask a learner to underline the adjective(s), e.g. *Football players are very <u>fit</u>. / Tai-chi isn't <u>dangerous</u> and it is <u>good</u> for the mind and the body.* Focus on the *Adjectives* explanation box, highlighting the position of adjectives in the two examples: before a noun or after a form of *be*, e.g. *is/are*. Point out that adjectives may come after *not* in negative sentences, e.g. *Tai-chi is not / isn't dangerous.*

4 👤 Focus on the adjectives in the box and their opposites in the table. Learners match them and write the words from the box in the correct places in the table. Check answers with the class. Some learners may know that *hard*

(= *not easy to bend or break* or *difficult*) can be the opposite of *soft* or *easy*.

Answers

hard	soft/easy
exciting	boring
dangerous	safe
expensive	cheap
difficult	easy
popular	unpopular
famous	unknown

Language note

You could highlight the negative prefix *un-* (= *not*) in *unknown* and *unpopular*. This might help learners remember the meanings.

CRITICAL THINKING

Go through the instructions with the class and focus on the writing task. Explain that the following sections of the unit will help them to prepare to write factual sentences about a popular sport in their country.

REMEMBER

Focus on the *Ideas maps* box. Tell learners that ideas maps are useful diagrams for helping us organize information and vocabulary. Focus on the ideas maps. Ask learners to look back at Reading 1 *The world's top five favourite sports* and notice that each paragraph (1–5) there is shown on the ideas map here as a separate part of the diagram. You could demonstrate how the ideas map can be gradually built up by drawing the central topic 'bubble' containing 'Top 5 Sports' and adding the separate sections branching off it.

CREATE

1 　Tell learners that they are going to make their own ideas map for Reading 2 *Sport in Brazil: Watch, Play, Learn!* Ask them to look back at the Reading 2 text and find the key information, words (mainly nouns and adjectives) and numbers associated with each sport. Ask them to work with a partner to create their ideas maps using *The world's top five favourite sports* example as a model. Pairs can either create one ideas map together or each produce copies of the same ideas map; they can either use the ideas map

outline in the Student's Book or a separate sheet of paper/electronic device. Tell them to use different colours for different sets of information. Monitor and give help/vocabulary where needed.

Answers

The *Sport in Brazil* ideas maps could include any of the following information:
1) Football: adults and children play: on football field / on the beach / in the street; world-famous footballers: Pelé, Kaka, Ronaldinho; 13 million players; 29,208 clubs
2) Capoeira: mix of martial arts, exercise + music: do in groups – in the park or in the street; people go to Brazil to learn it
3) Motor racing: famous Formula 1 drivers: Piquet, Senna, Massa; watch on TV / in São Paulo / at Interlagos Speedway.

2 　Focus on the Ideas map checklist and make sure learners understand what they need to check. Learners check their ideas maps and make any corrections. Ask learners if they could use their ideas maps to write a text including all the ideas ideas in the reading text. Discuss the ideas ideas in the reading text with the class. If learners think they have left anything out, they could add it to their ideas maps now.

3 　Collect the ideas maps and display them round the classroom for learners to look at. Encourage them to comment, e.g. *Which are the most colourful? Which are well organized? Do they all contain the same information? What differences do you notice?*

WRITING

GRAMMAR FOR WRITING

Subject – verb – adjective

Focus on the *Subject – Verb – Adjective* explanation box. This box highlights the normal word order of sentences using the linking verb *be*: a subject (noun / noun phrase / pronoun) – a form of the verb *be* (*am/is/are*) – a noun / noun phrase or an adjective. Point out that the verb may be negative here, e.g. *am/is/are not*.

Language note

The types of sentences highlighted in the explanation box are sentences using the linking verb *be*, which is followed by a complement, i.e. a noun/noun phrase or an adjective, not an object. These sentences give more information about the subject rather than describing an action or event.

1 👤👥 Focus on the sentences and elicit a couple of answers from learners as examples. Learners circle the options that are true for them. Ask learners to compare their sentences with a partner and note how many answers are the same. Ask if any pairs agreed on every statement.

Answers
Answers will vary.

Optional activity

Read out both alternatives for the statements in Exercise 1 and ask for a show of hands for each. Write the results on the board and have a class discussion about one or two of the statements.

2 👤 Focus on the jumbled sentences. Learners put the words in order. Remind them that the first word has an initial capital letter. Check answers with the class.

Answers
1 Ice hockey is popular in Russia.
2 Minoru Iwata is a famous baseball player in Japan.
3 Basketball is not popular in my country.
4 Tickets for football are cheap.
5 It is difficult to buy tickets for tennis.

Subject – Verb – Adverb

Revise prepositional phrases (from Unit 2) by eliciting some examples of these and putting them on the board. Go through the *Subject – Verb – Adverb* explanation box with learners, then ask them to decide if the phrases you wrote on the board describe *when* (time) or *where* (place).

Language note

Notice that some of the example sentences in the explanation box contain an object, e.g. *Faisal plays **tennis** on Wednesday* and some do not: *I go running in the park*.

3 👤 Focus on the sentences and explain the instructions. Elicit the first answer as an

example. Learners underline the remaining prepositional phrases. Check answers with the class.

Answers
1 I play tennis <u>on Monday and Wednesday</u>. T
2 <u>In summer</u>, we go horse-riding. T
3 I watch Arsenal football club <u>in the stadium</u>. P
4 Children go ice skating <u>on the lake</u>. P
5 Many people play volleyball <u>on the beach</u>. P
6 I do judo <u>on Sunday evening</u>. T
7 <u>In winter</u>, we go skiing. T
8 Ahmed goes surfing <u>in the morning</u>. T

4 👤 Ask learners to decide if the underlined phrases in Exercise 3 are prepositional phrases of time (T) or place (P). Again, elicit the first answer as an example. Learners mark the remaining sentences (T) or (P). Check answers with the class.

Answers
See Exercise 3.

5 👤 Explain that there is an incorrect preposition in each prepositional phrase in these sentences. Revise the use of *on* with days of the week and *in* with seasons from Units 2 and 3 if necessary. Elicit the first answer as an example. Learners find the prepositions and correct them. Check answers with the class.

Answers
1 People play tennis <u>in</u> the park.
2 Football games are <u>on</u> Wednesday evening.
3 Children play football <u>on</u> the beach.
4 <u>In</u> spring, we play baseball.
5 I do exercise <u>on</u> Monday.

ACADEMIC WRITING SKILLS

Commas

Start by revising the use of commas for separating a prepositional phrase at the beginning of a sentence (Unit 2). Write an example of such a sentence on the board and ask learners where the comma should go, e.g. *In the afternoons we play football.*

Focus on the *Commas* explanation box: the revision point about a comma separating a prepositional phrase and the new point about its use to separate two nouns in a list. Give another example of the second type of sentence, e.g. *Tomiko plays tennis, football and basketball.*

Write it on the board without commas and ask a learner to write in the comma(s).

1 👤👥 If necessary, briefly revise the rules for capital letters and full stops in sentences. Demonstrate the exercise by writing the first one on the board and correcting it together. Ask learners to correct the punctuation in the sentences; they can then check their answers in pairs. Check answers with the class.

> **Answers**
>
> 1 Ayrton Senna was a famous driver from Brazil.
> 2 In winter, the children go ice skating.
> 3 In summer, we go swimming in the river.
> 4 In May, June, July and August we play baseball.
> 5 John does karate in the park.

SPELLING

2 👤 Learners rearrange the letters to make the names of sports. They can use the glossary on page 197 if necessary. Check answers with the class.

> **Answers**
>
> 1 football 2 basketball 3 tennis 4 hockey
> 5 baseball

> **Optional activity**
>
> 👥👥 Make this activity competitive by putting the learners into teams and giving them a time limit of 15 seconds to rearrange each set of letters. When the time limit is up, go round each group and get them to show you the correct word. Each team with the word spelled correctly within the time limit receives one point.

3 👤 Learners rearrange the letters to make the names of countries, using the initial capital to help them. Check answers with the class.

> **Answers**
>
> 1 Turkey 2 Taiwan 3 China 4 Japan 5 Brazil
> 6 Chile 7 South Korea 8 United Arab Emirates

WRITING TASK

PLAN

1 👤 Ask learners to choose a popular sport in their country and make a ideas map for it. Ask them to look at the mind ideas in the Critical thinking section for ideas. Encourage learners

to include the following information: the name of the sport, the people who like the sport (e.g. type of people, age, sex, number, etc.); the places people do/play the sport; the times of day or seasons when people play/do the sport; the names of famous sportsmen or women in the sport; how many people/fans watch the sport; where you can see the sport; the price of tickets. Suggest learners give suitable headings to each section to help them organize their writing, e.g. *Who/People, Where/Places, When/Times, Famous players, Watching the sport.* Encourage them to use dictionaries to find unknown vocabulary and monitor and help as needed.

WRITE A FIRST DRAFT

2 👤 Learners complete the sentence with answers that are true for the sport they have chosen. You could write an example as a model on the board,
e.g. *Cricket is very popular in India.*

3 👤 Learners use their ideas map and the prompts to write further sentences about their chosen sport. They should copy the completed gapped sentence from Exercise 2 into their notebooks first as an introduction.

EDIT

4 and 5 👤 Focus on the task checklist. Go through the checklist to make sure learners know what to check. Then ask the learners to edit their work, using the checklist to help them. You can ask learners to produce a final draft of their work before handing it in. If not, collect in their edited first draft to mark and correct. If the writing task has produced some common errors, highlight these in later lessons, using the model answer to give examples. Choose some good examples of writing from individual learners and ask them if you can share them with the class. These could be displayed on the walls of the classroom for the others to read, projected onto the board or photocopied and given out.

> **Answers**
>
> See page 134 for a model answer.

Optional activity

Ask learners to identify similarities and differences between their own work and the model answer and the *Sport in Brazil* text. Ask learners to underline or highlight a particular language feature from the unit (e.g. *do, play* and *go* verb + noun collocations, prepositional phrases, adjectives before nouns and after *is* and *are*, commas following prepositional phrases at the start of sentences and between two nouns in a list) first in their own work and then in the model answer or *Sport in Brazil*. Provide feedback by discussing the examples of the target language as a class and writing them on the board. You could also choose some good examples from the learners' own work to share with the class.

OBJECTIVES REVIEW

See Introduction, page 9, for ideas about using the Objectives Review with your learners.

WORDLIST

See Introduction, page 9, for ideas about how to make the most of the Wordlist with your learners.

REVIEW TEST

See page 111 for the photocopiable Review Test for this unit and page 94, for ideas about when and how to administer the Review Test.

RESEARCH PROJECT

Organize your own sports competition.

Divide the class and ask them to find out about different types of sports. They do not have to be traditional and can even include new or unusual sports. Tell the learners that they will need to organize a major sports competition. The first stage of the sports event is to educate different people about the benefits of each sport played. Learners can do this by producing posters for display in their learning environment.

Learners then need to find a way to encourage people to take part in the competition in a poster presentation to the class. The class can decide which competition is the most suitable for their country or region

6 JOBS

Learning objectives

Go through the learning objectives with the class to make sure everyone understands what they can expect to achieve in this unit. Point out that learners will have a chance to review these objectives again at the end of the unit.

UNLOCK YOUR KNOWLEDGE

Lead-in

👤 Ask: *How many jobs do you know in English?* Give learners one minute to write down as many jobs as they can (see jobs vocabulary in the wordlist for this unit). For feedback, ask how many they wrote down and ask one or two pairs to share their lists with the class. Ask if anyone has a job that no one has mentioned yet.

👤 Focus on the wordbox and the gapped sentences. Learners complete the sentences with the correct words, using a dictionary if necessary. Check answers with the class.

> **Answers**
> 1 manager 2 architect 3 nurse 4 software engineer 5 primary school teacher

WATCH AND LISTEN

Optional activity

Focus on the video stills at the top of the page and ask learners to say what they can see. Use the pictures to check understanding of *bicycle* and *train* (n).

PREPARING TO WATCH

UNDERSTANDING KEY VOCABULARY

1 👤 Ask learners to read the sentences and complete them with the words in the box, using the glossary on page 198 to help them. Check answers with the class. Elicit other examples of rooms and symbols, e.g. star, arrow. Model and drill the pronunciation of any difficult words, e.g. *symbol* /ˈsɪmbəl/, *deliver* /dɪˈlɪvə/, *lunch* /lʌntʃ/, *kitchen* /ˈkɪtʃɪn/ and *paint* /peɪnt/. Learners may already know *cook* (v) but not as a noun (see Language note) so highlight this now.

> **Answers**
> 1 cook 2 paint 3 lunch 4 deliver 5 symbol
> 6 kitchen

WHILE WATCHING

UNDERSTANDING MAIN IDEAS

2 ▶️👤👥 Focus on the two questions and multiple-choice answers. Play the video. Learners watch, then circle the correct options. After viewing, allow learners to discuss their answers in pairs. Check answers with the class. Ask: *What is a dabbawalla? (a person who delivers lunch in Mumbai)*

> **Answers**
> 1 a 2 b

Video script

India. Mumbai. This is a very busy city. The roads are crowded with people and bicycles; cars and animals. Mumbai is an important city. There are many big companies and offices here.

The man on the bicycle is a 'dabbawalla'. A dabbawalla takes food to people in offices.

More than 200,000 workers in Mumbai want home-cooked food. Dabbawallas take food from small kitchens like this and deliver it to businesses and offices in the city. Cooks put the food into a tiffin tin – a special type of lunchbox.

The dabbawallas take the tiffin tins to the train station.

The dabbawallas put the tins in coloured bags or they paint symbols on the tins. The colours and symbols show them where to take each lunch. They put the lunches on the correct trains so they go to the correct person.

The dabbawallas go by train, bicycle and on foot to deliver the lunches. There are about 5,000 dabbawallas in Mumbai. The dabbawallas work very well. There is only one mistake in every 8 million deliveries.

LISTENING FOR KEY INFORMATION

3 ▶ 👤👥 Focus on the notes about the video and the different options. Use the video still on page 106 and elicit the meaning of *tiffin tin* (= the special tin for the lunches). Play the video. Elicit the correct answer for the first option. Play the video again if necessary. Learners choose the remaining correct options. After viewing, allow learners to discuss their answers in pairs. Check answers with the class.

> **Answers**
>
> 1 office workers 2 Cooks 3 train 4 paint symbols
> 5 5,000

> **Background note**
>
> India, officially the Republic of India, is a country in South Asia. It is the world's largest democracy and second most populous country with a population of approximately 1.2 billion. The major languages are Hindi, English and more than 20 other official languages. The capital city is New Delhi and the most populated city is Mumbai on the west coast. The literal meaning of dabbawalla is 'box person', named after the lunch boxes (tiffin tins) they carry.

DISCUSSION

4 👥 Learners discuss the questions in pairs. Monitor and make a note of any interesting comments, e.g. views on the difficulty of the dabbawallas' job, examples of food delivery services. Conduct full class feedback and ask individual learners to share their ideas with the class. Use this opportunity to extend the discussion and encourage learners to produce more complex sentences, e.g. *What kind of food do people deliver in your country (sandwiches, pizzas)? Would you like a dabbawalla to deliver your lunch?*

READING 1

PREPARING TO READ

PREVIEWING

1 👤 Ask learners to preview the three reading texts as quickly as possible to find out where they are from, then circle the correct option. Check answer with the class.

> **Answers**
>
> b

UNDERSTANDING KEY VOCABULARY

2 👤 Focus on the sentences and elicit the first answer as an example. Learners match the remaining sentences. Check answers with the class. Check understanding of new words by giving and eliciting personalized examples, e.g. *A teacher's salary is very small – not $120,000 a year!* Elicit another word for *trains* (*teaches*); note that two meanings for *train* are included in this unit (noun = *transport*; verb = *teach*). Model and drill pronunciation of any difficult words, e.g. *employer* /ɪmˈplɔɪə/, *salary* /ˈsæləri/ and *experience* /ɪkˈspɪəriənts/.

> **Answers**
>
> 1 c 2 d 3 b 4 a

3 👤 Ask learners to read the sentences and complete them with the words in the box, using the glossary on page 198. Check answers with the class and model and drill the pronunciation of *friendly* /ˈfrendli/ and *fluent* /ˈfluːənt/ if necessary. Check understanding of the new words with further questions and personalized examples, e.g. *What other food is healthy? Do you know anyone with a full-time job?*

> **Answers**
>
> 1 healthy 2 fit 3 fluent 4 part-time 5 friendly
> 6 full-time

WHILE READING

SCANNING TO FIND INFORMATION

4 👤 Focus on the table and the questions in the left-hand column and point out that each of the columns refers to a different advertisement. Check that learners can read the table and locate information by asking them to find some of the completed information, e.g. *pilot*, in the correct advertisement (B). From the information already in the table, learners should be able to work out that *location* = country. Elicit that the name of the employer is at the top of each advert. Elicit/pre-teach the meaning of *pilot* /ˈpaɪlət/. Complete the first gap with the class as an example, then learners work individually to scan the texts to complete the rest of the table. You can encourage them to scan quickly by setting a time limit appropriate to the ability level of your class. Check answers with the class.

| Answers
1 nurse 2 teacher 3 China 4 India 5 FlyHigh (air transport company) 6 200,000 INR per journey 7 320,000 JPY per month 8 FT

Background note

The Chinese Yuan Renminbi (CNY) is the currency of China.
The Indian Rupee (INR) is the currency of India.
The Japanese Yen (JPY) is the currency of Japan.

READING FOR DETAIL

5   Focus on the *Reading for detail* box. Remind learners of reading techniques they have encountered so far, i.e. asking themselves questions, scanning a text quickly for key words relevant to their questions and then reading closely once they have located the right section of the text.

Focus on the statements in Exercise 5 and elicit the first answer as an example. Briefly check understanding of *have to* and *must* = it is necessary or very important. Learners should be able to deduce that *staff* in advert C = *teachers* in question 4 but may need help here. Elicit the meaning of *10 years' experience = has worked as (job) for 10 years*. Check answers with the class.

| Answers
1 T 2 F 3 T 4 T 5 F 6 T

READING BETWEEN THE LINES

WORKING OUT MEANING FROM CONTEXT

6   Explain that we can often work out the meaning of an unknown word by using the information around the word (= the context) or our existing knowledge of a topic. Ask learners to find the words in the box in texts A–C and underline them wherever they find them.

Model and drill pronunciation of *location* /ləʊˈkeɪʃən/, *applicant* /ˈæplɪkənt/, *education* /ˌedjʊˈkeɪʃən/ and *medicine* /ˈmedɪsən/.

7   Ask learners to complete the definitions with the words from Exercise 6, using the context of the underlined words in texts A–C to help them. Elicit the first answer as an example. Check answers with the class.

| Answers
1 medicine 2 education 3 location 4 applicant

DISCUSSION

8 Learners discuss the questions in pairs. Monitor and make a note of any interesting comments.

READING 2

PREPARING TO READ

UNDERSTANDING KEY VOCABULARY

1   Focus on the wordbox and the gapped sentences. Learners complete the sentences using a dictionary. Check answers with the class. Check understanding by giving/eliciting further examples and personalizing these where possible, e.g. *Do you know any great computer games? Do you know any bad ones?* Model and drill pronunciation of *soon* /suːn/, *fitness instructor* /ˈfɪtnəs ɪnˈstrʌktə/, *great* /greɪt/, *apply* /əˈplaɪ/, *hour* /aʊə/ and *gym* /dʒɪm/.

| Answers
1 great 2 link 3 soon 4 apply 5 fitness instructor 6 long hours 7 gym

WHILE READING

SCANNING TO FIND INFORMATION

2   Focus on the gapped sentences and elicit what sort of information learners need to find (the job described in each email). Check that they know where to look each time, i.e. quickly find the name from each sentence at the beginning of the correct email and then scan that email for a job name.

Set a short time limit to ensure that learners scan read the texts. Check answers with the class.

Answers

1 fitness instructor 2 software engineer 3 teacher

3 👤 Learners follow the same strategy to find the location for each job. Again, set a short time limit, then check answers with the class.

Answers

1 Manchester (UK)
2 Oslo (Norway)
3 Yeonggwang (South Korea)

4 👤 Focus on sentence 1 and elicit which email (Daria's) and which key word (*grades*) learners should look for to find the missing information. Learners complete the sentences. Once again, set a time limit so that learners don't spend too long reading closely. Check answers with the class. Elicit the meaning of *per* in *per month* (= *every*).

Answers

1 10, 12
2 12
3 4,150

READING FOR DETAIL

5 👤 Focus on the statements. Ask learners to read the texts for detail this time, then match the statements to the correct emails by writing the correct initials. Check answers with the class. Elicit other ways of saying *good with people* = *friendly*, *likes people*. Ask: *Are you good with people? Do you get up early?* etc. to personalize the language.

Answers

1 C 2 D 3 E 4 C 5 D

DISCUSSION

6 👥 Learners discuss the questions in pairs. Monitor and make a note of any interesting comments you hear, e.g. the most popular jobs with young people. Conduct full class feedback and ask individual learners to share their ideas with the class. Ask learners to give reasons for their choices for and against certain jobs using vocabulary from the unit, e.g. big/small salaries, long hours, not full time, nice location, have to get up early, etc.

⊙ LANGUAGE DEVELOPMENT

VOCABULARY FOR JOBS

1 👤 Focus on the table and highlight column A, which lists different jobs, and column B, which is for listing the activities of those jobs. Focus on the phrases in the wordbox and check learners' understanding of the phrasal verbs, e.g. *look after* = to take care of or be in charge of someone or something; *put out* = to stop something from burning. Elicit the first answer as an example. Ask learners to complete column B with the verb phrases from the box. Check answers with the class. You could personalize the new vocabulary by asking questions, e.g. *Is anyone in your family a …?* Model and drill pronunciation of *chef* /ʃef/, *flight attendant* /flaɪt əˈtendənt/, *accountant* /əˈkaʊntənt/, *actor* /ˈæktə/ and *director* /daɪˈrektə/. Ask: *What's another word for a chef?* (= a cook).

Answers

See Exercise 2.

> **Language note**
>
> Phrasal verbs, also called multiword verbs, consist of a verb and a particle, e.g. an adverb and/or a preposition. These verbs have a single meaning which is often completely different from the meaning of the individual words.

2 👤 Focus on column C of the table, which shows typical locations for the jobs. Ask learners to complete column C with the prepositional phrases from the box. Remind them to use full stops. Check answers with the class. Model and drill pronunciation of *restaurant* /ˈrestrɒnt/ and *movie* /ˈmuːvi/.

Answers

A jobs	B activities	C locations
1 A vet	looks after animals	in farms and zoos.
2 A manager	manages people	in an office.
3 A doctor	gives people medicine	in hospital.
4 A builder	builds houses	in towns and cities.
5 An accountant	looks after money	in a company.
6 A chef	prepares food	in a restaurant.
7 A fireman	puts out fires	in towns and cities.
8 A flight attendant	looks after passengers	on a plane.
9 An actor	plays a character	in a movie.
10 A film director	makes movies	in different countries.

Adjective phrases

Focus on the *Adjective phrases* explanation box. Explain that adjective phrases can follow a form of the verb *be*, e.g. *am (not), is (not), are (not)*, and give more information about the subject of a sentence. Highlight the three patterns on the board:

very + an adjective
an adjective + *and* + an adjective
good at + a noun, or *good with* + a noun

Optional activity

Elicit similar examples from learners by substituting different job titles and different adjectives for those in the *Adjective phrases* box:

(job) *must be* (*very* + adjective)
(job) *must be* (adjective + adjective)
(job) *must be* (*good at* + noun)

Write other jobs and adjectives on the board for learners to make more example sentences. Encourage fast finishers to give reasons for their choices, e.g. *Builders have to be healthy because they work outside.*

jobs	adjectives	nouns
Doctors Builders Firemen Flight attendants	intelligent kind fit healthy helpful	Maths people

3 Focus on sentences (1–10). Learners circle the best words and phrases to complete them. Demonstrate the activity by doing the first answer together as a class and discussing it. Point out that the exercise requires the '*best* words or phrases' so the alternatives won't be wrong. Check answers and discuss them as a class.

Answers

1 fit and strong
2 kind and patient
3 good with people
4 very intelligent
5 good with computers
6 good at Maths
7 polite and friendly
8 creative
9 beautiful
10 good with food

Language note

For questions 1 and 10, some learners may know the US English meaning of *smart* (= *intelligent*) and some the UK meaning (= *clean, tidy and well dressed*). The British English meaning is used here.

CRITICAL THINKING

Go through the instructions with the class and focus on the writing task. Explain that the following sections of the unit will help them to prepare to write sentences describing a job for a friend.

UNDERSTAND

Questionnaires

Focus on the *Questionnaires* explanation box. Explain how a Likert scale works, by highlighting the numbered responses from 1 = strongly disagree through to 5 = strongly agree. Check understanding of these phrases by writing them on a cline on the board. You could also draw emoticons or tick/cross symbols next to each phrase (e.g. ✓✓ = strongly agree, ✓ = agree, 0 = neither agree nor disagree, ✗ = disagree and ✗✗ = strongly disagree). Erase the phrases and elicit them from the learners by pointing to the symbols.

Background note

Questionnaires are often used by companies, service providers and institutions to carry out research. They usually include a series of questions and/or other prompts to gather information from respondents. Questionnaires are an economical way of gathering information which is then easy to compile. A Likert scale is named after the psychologist Rensis Likert (1903–1981), its inventor.

1 👤 Demonstrate the activity by doing the first one or two questions yourself as an example. Learners complete the questionnaire.

Answers

Answers will vary.

APPLY

2 👥 Learners read their partner's answers to the questionnaire and choose the best job for them from the box. Ask two or three pairs to tell the class which jobs they chose and why. Ask the partner to comment on how suitable they think the choice is for them.

WRITING

GRAMMAR FOR WRITING

Must and *have to*

Focus on the *must* and *have to* explanation box. Highlight the similar meanings (e.g. necessity) but different forms (e.g. *must* + infinitive, *have to* + infinitive). Point out here that *must* always has the same form and does not take -s in the third person singular. Contrast this with *have to* which does change (*has to*).

Language note

Modal auxiliary verbs are used with main verbs to indicate possibility, necessity, etc. These verbs are: *can, could, may, might, must, will, would, shall* and *should*. These verbs do not change form and are followed by the infinitive forms (without *to*) of other verbs. The verb *ought* is considered a modal verb but is followed by *to* + infinitive. Semi-modals can be used as modals but they have different forms. They include: *need, dare, had better* and *used to*. The verb *have (got) to* can be used like *must* but its form changes in the third person singular (e.g. *He has (got) to leave early*).

1 👤👥 Focus on the sentences. Learners find the errors and correct them. They can refer to the *must* and *have to* explanation box if necessary. Encourage fast finishers to compare their answers in pairs before checking with the class.

Answers

1 A builder <u>must</u> be strong and healthy.
2 <u>Firemen</u> have <u>to</u> work long hours.
3 A manager <u>has</u> to be helpful.
4 Teachers must <u>be</u> patient.
5 A software engineer must <u>to be</u> good at Maths.
6 Vets have <u>to be</u> good with animals.
7 An architect must <u>to be</u> creative.
8 An actor <u>must to</u> play a character in a movie.

have to

Focus on the *have to* explanation box. Point out that *do/does not have to* means that something is not necessary. In the examples, something is not necessary in order to do a particular job. Make clear that *must not* + infinitive has a different meaning, i.e. something is not allowed or is prohibited, e.g. *You must not smoke here.*

Optional activity

Write some prompts on the board for learners to make into sentences using *do/does not have to*, e.g.
Firemen / beautiful. → *Firemen don't have to be beautiful.*
A software engineer / good with food.
A student / kind and patient.
Nurses / good with animals.

You could turn this into a card game. Write jobs on one set of cards and adjectives/adjective phrases on another set of cards. Learners pick up one card from each pile and make a sentence using *must/have to* or *don't/doesn't have to*.

2 👤 Learners put the words in the correct order to make sentences. Check answers with the class.

Answers

1 An architect does not have to build houses.
2 A manager does not have to be kind and patient.
3 Nurses do not have to be good with computers.
4 Actors do not have to be smart.
5 A French teacher does not have to be good at Maths. / A Maths teacher does not have to be good at French.
6 A doctor does not have to be strong.

Joining sentences with *and*

Focus on the *Joining sentences with and* explanation box. Write the examples on the board to show how the sentences can be joined and repeated items deleted. Point out that you are just deleting repeated words (the same subject and the same verb) and that this doesn't change the meaning. Write another example on the board, e.g. *Primary school teachers have to be very kind. Primary school teachers have to be good with children.* Ask learners to identify the repeated subject and verb and make the deletions and the join with *and*.

3 👤 Elicit the first sentence as an example. Learners then join the sentences to make one sentence with *and*. Check answers with the class.

> **Answers**
>
> 1 Applicants must be smart and polite.
> 2 You do not have to be fit and strong.
> 3 Firemen have to be fit and healthy.
> 4 Daria has to teach English and French.

ACADEMIC WRITING SKILLS

SPELLING

Contractions

Focus on the *Contractions* explanation box. Show learners how the full forms change by writing them on the board, erasing the omitted letters and adding apostrophes. Model and drill pronunciation of the contractions:

> **I'm** a doctor. /aɪm/
>
> **Philip's** an engineer. /ˈfɪlɪps/
>
> **They're** architects. /ðeər/
>
> You **don't** have to be good at Maths. /dəʊnt/
>
> She **doesn't** have to be strong. /ˈdʌzənt/

You could also ask individual learners to change the contractions back to full forms on the board as preparation for the next exercise.

👤 Ask learners to rewrite the sentences with no contractions. Check answers with the class.

> **Answers**
>
> 1 I am very happy.
> 2 Daria is a serious teacher.
> 3 Hamdan is a good friend.
> 4 I hope you are well.
> 5 You do not have to work on Friday.

> **Language note**
>
> We do not usually use contractions in academic writing, such as essays, reports, non-fiction books, textbooks, journal articles and online articles. We can use contractions in informal writing, e.g. emails and letters to friends, online messaging and Twitter.

WRITING TASK

WRITE A FIRST DRAFT

1 👤 Ask learners to look back at the job they chose for their partners based on the questionnaire results. Tell them that they are now going to write an email to their partner describing this job. Ask if this email is formal or informal (informal) and whether contractions will be used in this writing or not (yes).

Focus learners on the writing frame in the email in their books. Read through the email together, making sure they understand the prompts and the type of information to include. They can refer back to earlier lessons in the unit for ideas and useful language. For the following jobs, direct learners to the emails in Reading 2 earlier in the unit: *fitness instructor, software engineer, teacher* (for a teacher, there is also the Reading 1 webpage). For the remaining jobs, direct learners to the *Vocabulary for jobs table* earlier in the unit: *manager, doctor, actor, vet*. Learners will need to invent a salary for the job as well as choose a location for it and decide whether it is full-or part-time. They could research similar jobs, their locations and salaries on the Internet if they wish.

Ask learners to complete the email to their partner. Encourage them to use dictionaries to find any vocabulary they need. Remind them to use *have to* and *must* to describe what sort of person the job advertiser is looking for. Monitor and help as required.

EDIT

2 and 3 👤 Focus on the task checklist. Go through the checklist to make sure learners know what to check. Then ask the learners to edit their work, using the checklist to help them. You can ask learners to produce a final draft of their work before handing it in. If not, collect in their edited first draft to mark and correct. If the writing task has produced some common errors, highlight these in later lessons, using the model answer to give examples.

Answers

See page 135 for a model answer.

Optional activity

After you have checked the first draft of the email, you could either ask learners to write up a neat copy or ask them to write an actual email. This could be sent to their partner and to you.

OBJECTIVES REVIEW

See Introduction, page 9, for ideas about using the Objectives Review with your learners.

WORDLIST

See Introduction, page 9, for ideas about how to make the most of the Wordlist with your learners.

REVIEW TEST

See page 114 for the photocopiable Review Test for this unit and page 94, for ideas about when and how to administer the Review Test.

RESEARCH PROJECT

Create your own CV.

This is an individual project. Tell learners that if they want a good job, then it is important to write a good CV. Inform the learners that CVs are often in paper form but in order to make theirs different, they are going to make theirs into a video or audio file. They may choose to make an animation using an online animation application if this is more appropriate.

Tell the learners to think about their skills, hobbies, educational history, qualifications and adjectives to describe themselves. They could also write their CV in a resume application as an alternative.

7 HOMES AND BUILDINGS

Learning objectives

Go through the learning objectives with the class to make sure everyone understands what they can expect to achieve in this unit. Point out that learners will have a chance to review these objectives again at the end of the unit.

UNLOCK YOUR KNOWLEDGE

Lead-in

👥 Ask: *Where are we now?* (in a college/school/university building). Ask learners to describe it (an old/modern/new/big/small building). *What do you think of this building?* Then ask: *How many different buildings were you in/did you go into yesterday?* Give learners one minute to write down as many buildings as they can. For feedback, ask them how many they wrote down and get one or two pairs to share their lists with the class. These could include: *house, apartment (US) or flat (UK), bus or train station, shopping mall/centre, school, shop, restaurant, leisure centre, library, post office.*

👥 Focus on the three questions. Learners ask and answer them in pairs. If they have access to the Internet in the classroom, they could research tall buildings in their city and find out how tall these buildings are. Ask one or two pairs to report back to the class.

WATCH AND LISTEN

Optional activity

Focus on the video stills at the top of the page and ask learners to say what they can see.

PREPARING TO WATCH

USING YOUR KNOWLEDGE TO PREDICT CONTENT

1 👤 Check learners' understanding of the four statements, especially the comparatives in question 3. You could do this by writing pairs of numbers on the board to elicit *smaller than / the same as / bigger than*. Check the meaning of *needs* (= must have) and revise

population by eliciting another way to say this (= all the people living somewhere). Check pronunciation of numbers and years, e.g. *eight million* /ˈmɪljən/, *nineteen ninety*. Learners choose the correct options; point out that they will need to use their existing knowledge to do this but they may need to guess some of the answers. Using their existing knowledge and guessing in advance will help prepare them to understand the video better. Learners will check their answers in Exercise 4.

> **Answers**
> See Exercise 4 below.

UNDERSTANDING KEY VOCABULARY

2 👤 Ask learners to look at the words in the table and check the meanings in the glossary on page 198. Check learners' understanding by asking questions, e.g. *What do you do in a ...?* Elicit sentences using some of the words about the learners' home town/city. Model and drill pronunciation of any difficult new words, e.g. *shopping mall* /ˈʃɒpɪŋ mɔːl/.

USING VISUALS TO PREDICT CONTENT

3 ▶👤 Play the video with no sound. Learners put a tick next to the things they see in column A of the table in Exercise 2. Check answers with the class.

> **Answers**
> swimming pool, restaurants, traffic, park, lights, apartments

WHILE WATCHING

UNDERSTANDING MAIN IDEAS

4 ▶👤 Play the video with sound. Learners listen and check their answers to Exercise 1. Check answers with the class. Elicit China's capital city (Beijing). Ask: *What was the population of Shanghai in 1990?* (around 14 million)

> **Answers**
> 1 b 2 c 3 c 4 a

Background note

Shanghai is a city in eastern China, located on the Yangtze River and Chinese coast. Although it is not the capital, it is the largest city by population in the world. It is an important financial centre and one of the busiest ports in the world.

LISTENING FOR KEY INFORMATION

5 ▶️ 🧍 Play the video again. Learners listen and put a tick next to the things they hear in column B. Check answers with the class.

> ### Answers
>
> swimming pool, traffic, park, offices, leisure centre, lights, apartments

Video script

Today, cities are even bigger, busier and more exciting. The buildings are taller, the lights are brighter and there is more traffic.

This is Shanghai. In 1990, around 14 million people lived here. Now, there are more than 23 million!

It is important to build more homes here – and fast! These men work at night. They are building apartments.

This is Vincent Lo. He is from Hong Kong. Vincent's company makes buildings in every part of China. Today Vincent is looking at a new project in Shanghai.

Vincent: Over here, we'll have a swimming pool and a leisure centre. This is the view. Over there is a park and a lake. And here are offices.

Vincent's company built Xintiandi. Xintiandi means 'New heaven and earth'. It is a new part of Shanghai. The man with Vincent is Ben Wood. He is an architect. He works for Vincent's company.

People like Vincent and Ben are working all over China to build similar places to live.

DISCUSSION

6 👥 Learners work in pairs to ask and answer the questions. With stronger classes / fast finishers, ask the following questions, which they could research using the Internet: *What is the population of your city? Is the population today the same as in 1990? What is the biggest city in your country? What is the capital city? Is there a lot of traffic in your city? When is it busy? Do you go to the shopping mall / leisure centre? How often? What do you do there?* Ask one or two pairs to report back to the class.

READING 1

PREPARING TO READ

UNDERSTANDING KEY VOCABULARY

1 🧍 👥 Focus on the table. Check understanding of *inside* and *outside* and the pronunciation of *material* /mə'tɪəriəl/. Elicit some simple examples that learners may know for each heading, e.g. room names or furniture for 'things inside a house', etc. Elicit the correct place in the table for *roof*. Learners complete the table with the other words, then check their answers in pairs. Remind them that for some words, more than one answer is possible. Check answers with the class and model and drill any difficult pronunciation, e.g. *ceiling* /'siːlɪŋ/, *mirror* /'mɪrə/ and *narrow* /'nærəʊ/.

> ### Answers
>
> things inside a house: ceiling, wall, room, window, mirror
> things outside a house: roof, garden, wall, window
> adjectives to describe a house: tall, narrow
> materials: glass, plastic, metal

USING VISUALS TO PREDICT CONTENT

Remind learners that we can use pictures, etc. to help us understand what a text is about. Focus on the *Using visuals to predict content* box. You could sketch examples of a *graph* and a *table* on the board to ensure learners understand these terms. Alternatively, show learners some real newspapers and magazines and ask them to predict the content of some of the articles by looking at the visuals in those.

2 🧍 Focus on the statement and phrases (a–d). Check understanding and pronunciation of: *creative* /kri'eɪtɪv/ (= using new and unusual ideas, not traditional); *expensive* /ɪk'spensɪv/ (= costing a lot of money); *environmentally friendly* /ɪn,vaɪrən'mentəli 'frendli/ (harmful to the air, water and land where people, animals and plants live). Ask learners to look at the photographs in Reading text 1, then circle the phrases they agree with. Discuss the answers with the whole class and encourage learners to give their reasons.

> ### Answers
>
> Answers will vary, but students are likely to choose a and c.

WHILE READING

SCANNING TO FIND INFORMATION

3 👤👥 Focus on the table. Check learners understand the column headings; you could draw pictures on the board for *shape* and use the photograph for *steep*.

If necessary, revise scanning techniques and ask which words learners will scan for to locate the sections of the text which contain the answers (*Japanese* or *Japan*, *Vietnamese* or *Vietnam* and then the column heading words). Elicit the first answer as an example. Learners complete the rest of the table. Check answers with the class.

Answers

	windows are different shapes	has glass walls	has a small garden on the roof	rooms are narrow
Japanese steep roof house	✓			✓
Vietnamese 'garden home'		✓	✓	

READING FOR DETAIL

4 👤 Focus on the statements. Learners read the text again more closely and mark the statements as true or false. Check answers with the class and ask learners to read out the sentence in the text where they found each answer. You could ask fast finishers / more able learners to correct the false statements.

Answers

1 F Professor Chan's favourite home designs are Japanese.
2 T
3 F Professor Chan says it is important to build houses that are environmentally friendly.
4 T
5 T
6 F In Amsterdam, one architect put mirrors on the walls.

Optional activity

👥 Give learners the following questions to answer in pairs:

Which house design from the magazine do you prefer? Why?

What are popular building materials in your country? (Pre-teach some building materials for this if necessary, e.g. *concrete, brick, wood*, etc.)

What styles of house, e.g. apartments, houses, are popular in your country?

Ask one or two pairs to report back to the class.

READING 2

PREPARING TO READ

PREVIEWING

1 👤 Focus on statements. Learners quickly preview the text and the picture and circle the correct options. Check answers with the class.

Answers

1 encyclopedia 2 tall building 3 students

UNDERSTANDING KEY VOCABULARY

2 👤 Focus on the wordbox and the gapped sentences. Learners complete the sentences with the words from the box, using the glossary on page 198 to help them. Check answers with the class. Elicit another way of saying *world-famous* (= known by many people in the world). Some learners may know *elevator* (US) for *lift* (UK). Elicit more sentences using the new words to provide personalized practice, e.g. *(name of building/place) is world-famous*.

Answers

1 open 2 modern 3 floor 4 lift 5 world-famous

WHILE READING

SCANNING TO FIND INFORMATION

3 👤 Focus on the table and the names of the three buildings. Ask questions to check learners can read the table information accurately, e.g. *Which country is Taipei 101 in? How many lifts does Burj Khalifa have?* Elicit the pronunciation and meaning of *UAE*

(United Arab Emirates) and *USD* (United States [American] dollars). Ask: *What does 'year' refer to in the table?*
(= the year the building opened).

Focus on the gaps and elicit ideas for the words/headings that will help learners find the missing information (the heading questions will help learners to find the information for gaps 4–6). Elicit the first answer as an example. Learners scan the text and complete the table. Check answers with the class.

> **Answers**
>
> 1 Dubai 2 492 3 509 4 101 5 31 6 1,760,000,000

UNDERSTANDING DISCOURSE

> **Language note**
>
> *Discourse* here refers to the way in which texts are constructed and the way sentences and meaning are connected together in a piece of writing.

Pronouns

Focus on the *Pronouns* explanation box. You can demonstrate the linking of pronouns back to nouns by putting the examples on the board and drawing arrows between the relevant words. Remind learners to look at whether the pronouns are singular or plural, and masculine, feminine or neuter (*it*). Remind learners to use pronouns in their own writing to avoid repetition and make their texts more fluent and natural.

4 Focus on the buildings in the box and the sentences. Learners can deduce the first answer but will need to look at the table or scan the reading text for the other answers. Check answers with the class.

> **Answers**
>
> 1 Taipei 101
> 2 Burj Khalifa
> 3 Taipei 101 and the Shanghai World Financial Center
> 4 Taipei 101

⊙ LANGUAGE DEVELOPMENT

VOCABULARY FOR BUILDINGS

1 Focus on the wordbox and the gapped sentences. Learners have already come across several of these words in the course: *library, museum, train station* (Unit 4), *stadium* (Unit 6) and *mall* (earlier in this unit). Point out the photograph of the ice rink at the Rockefeller Center on page 131. Learners complete the sentences. Check answers with the class.

> **Answers**
>
> 1 mall 2 Stadium 3 Hotel 4 cinema 5 train station
> 6 museum 7 ice rink 8 Library

VOCABULARY FOR PARTS OF BUILDINGS

2 Ask learners to read the sentences (1–5) and circle the correct words. Check answers with the class.

> **Answers**
>
> 1 car park 2 escalator 3 entrance 4 stairs 5 exit

ADJECTIVES

3 Ask learners to match the adjectives (1–6) to their opposites (a–f). Learners check their answers in pairs before you check answers with the whole class. Elicit sentences using the words from this exercise and Exercise 2 to check understanding and personalize the vocabulary, e.g. *Is the shopping mall in your city big/small/old/new? How many escalators are there at the shopping mall? How many entrances/exits/car parks are there?*

> **Answers**
>
> 1 d 2 c 3 e 4 f 5 b 6 a

CRITICAL THINKING (20 MINUTES)

Go through the instructions with the class and focus on the writing task. Explain that the following sections of the unit will help them to prepare to write a comparison of two buildings.

UNDERSTAND

Focus on the *Comparison of data* box. Explain that we can use *data* /ˈdeɪtə/ (= information in the form of facts and numbers) to analyze and compare things.

1   Focus on the table. Ask: *What does this table compare?* (shopping malls) *How many?* (four) *Which countries are they in?* (the USA, the UK, Turkey and the Philippines). Ask further questions to check understanding of the information in the table, e.g. *How many shops are there in the Country Club Plaza?* Focus on the wordbox and point out that the missing words in the table are the categories or headings for three rows of information. Revise *location* (from Unit 6). Learners write the words from the box in the correct gaps. Check answers with the class. Elicit the pronunciation of squared numbers in m^2 (= metres squared).

> **Answers**
> 1 location 2 year 3 size

> **Optional activity**
>
> Ask learners to make up (oral or written) questions for other learners to answer about the table now that it is complete, e.g. *How many … ? Where is …?*

ANALYZE

2   Demonstrate the activity by modelling the first one or two questions with a strong learner. Choose two shopping malls from Table 7.1 to compare. The learner asks you the first question about them and you answer, e.g. *The … is more modern.* Ask another open pair to ask and answer a question. Notice that the data for floors, restaurants and cinemas are the same for some of the shopping malls, so with a stronger class, you could pre-teach the following phrases: *… is the same as … , … has the same number as … .* Elicit some example sentences with these phrases using the information in the table, e.g. *Floors →*

The *Istanbul Cevahir* has the same number as the *SM Mall of Asia.* Cinemas → The *Country Club Plaza* is the same as the *Metro Centre.* Alternatively, you could just pre-teach the phrase: *They are the same.*

In pairs, learners ask and answer about their chosen malls. Monitor, making a note of any common errors or difficult areas, and discuss these at the end.

> **Answers**
> Answers will vary.

WRITING

GRAMMAR FOR WRITING

Comparing quantities

Focus on the *Comparing quantities* explanation box. Elicit further sentences using the form. For example, give different numbers of pens to pairs of learners and ask for sentences about them, e.g. *Fred has more pens than Ted.*

1   Focus on the jumbled sentences. Learners reorder the words and phrases to make sentences. Remind learners to look for the capital letters to find the first word in each sentence. Check answers with the class.

> **Answers**
> 1 The Burj Khalifa has more floors than Taipei 101.
> 2 The Louvre museum has more visitors than the British Museum.
> 3 The Istanbul Cevahir has more cinemas than the SM Mall of Asia.
> 4 The SM Mall of Asia has more restaurants than the Metro Centre.
> 5 The Metro Centre has more shops than the Country Club Plaza.

Comparative adjectives

Focus on the *Comparative adjectives* box. Explain that we use comparative adjectives to describe the differences between two things. Make sure learners understand the meaning of *syllable* by saying different words out loud and beating with your hand as you say each syllable. Say adjectives learners know and elicit the number of syllables in each.

Go through the different comparative forms and spelling rules. Make it clear that only -r is added if an adjective already ends in -e, e.g. *wide → wider*. Show -y changing to -ier, in e.g. *busy → busier*, on the board. Write adjectives with different numbers of syllables on the board and elicit their comparative forms, e.g. *new → newer, happy → happier, famous → more famous, dangerous → more dangerous*.

2 👤 Focus on the sentences. Explain that several sentences contain more than one error: missing words, incorrect words and some unnecessary words which need to be crossed out. You could demonstrate by correcting the first sentence with the whole class on the board. Check answers with the class.

> ### Answers
>
> 1 The Louvre museum is <u>more</u> popular <u>than</u> the British Museum.
> 2 The SM Mall of Asia is more ~~of~~ modern <u>than</u> the Istanbul Cevahir.
> 3 The Country Club Plaza is ~~more~~ <u>smaller</u> <u>than</u> the Istanbul Cevahir.
> 4 Modern buildings <u>are</u> <u>uglier</u> <u>than</u> historic buildings.
> 5 The SM Mall of Asia <u>is</u> taller <u>than</u> the Metro Centre.
> 6 Wood is more expensive <u>than</u> plastic.
> 7 This street is ~~many~~ <u>narrower</u> than the main road.
> 8 New York is ~~more~~ <u>busier</u> than Kansas City.

> ### Optional activity
>
> Learners write an adjective on a slip of paper and the name of two (local) places on two other separate slips. They give the slips to a partner and ask him/her to make a comparative sentence using the words. Encourage learners to think about meaning as well as grammatical accuracy. Alternatively, prepare a similar set of 'cards' before the lesson and give them to pairs to make sentences. Learners write their sentences out in full. Write good sentences on the board.

Joining sentences with *but*

Focus on the *Joining sentences with but* explanation box. You could use the board to show the way the new sentence is gradually built up. Ask learners to join two more similar sentences in the same way on the board. To prepare for the next exercise, demonstrate the same process with sentences that compare quantities, e.g. *The Burj Khalifa has more floors than Taipei 101. Taipei 101 has more lifts than the Burj Khalifa. → The Burj Khalifa has more floors than Taipei 101 but Taipei 101 has more lifts.*

> ### Language note
>
> The explanation box here deals with use of the conjunction *but* and ellipsis of repeated words to join sentences. The conjunction *but* is used to add a contrasting fact. It is a coordinating conjunction used to link clauses.
>
> Ellipsis is when words are omitted because they are obvious from the context. The second *than + noun / noun phrase* can be omitted because the meaning is clear without it.

3 👤 Focus on the pairs of sentences. If you have already asked learners to join sentences with *but* on the board, you can ask them to do the exercise straight away. If not, show how to join the first pair with the class as an example. Check answers with the class.

> ### Answers
>
> 1 The Metro Centre has more floors than the Country Club Plaza but the Country Club Plaza has more restaurants.
> 2 The Istanbul Cevahir has more cinemas than the SM Mall of Asia but the SM Mall of Asia has more shops.
> 3 The Metro Centre is more modern than the Country Club Plaza but the Country Club Plaza is bigger.
> 4 The SM Mall of Asia is bigger than the Country Club Plaza but the Country Club Plaza is older.

ACADEMIC WRITING SKILLS

Spelling: double consonants

Focus on the explanation box. Revise *vowel* and *consonant* if necessary by eliciting examples. Use the board to show how some comparative adjectives and some verb forms (-ing forms) repeat the last consonant of the base form of the adjective or the infinitive verb form (i.e. the consonant is doubled). Point out that all three of the bullet points here have to be true for the consonant to double.

1 👤 Focus on the text. Ask learners to read it through first, then correct the underlined words for spelling and missing capital letters. You could elicit the first correction as an example. Monitor and during feedback focus on any common errors learners missed and revise the forms/language. Check answers with the class.

Answers

What are <u>malls</u>?
Malls are big buildings for <u>shopping</u>. They are near big cities. Sometimes they are inside skyscrapers. Many cities have more than one mall. Malls have <u>restaurants</u> and <u>cinemas</u>. The <u>restaurants</u> are <u>bigger</u> than <u>restaurants</u> in the city. Some malls also have gyms and <u>swimming</u> pools.
The <u>Country Club Plaza</u> in <u>Kansas City</u> in the <u>United States</u> was the first mall in the world. It is popular today but there are <u>bigger</u> malls in <u>America</u>, <u>Europe</u>, the <u>Gulf</u> and <u>Asia</u>.

WRITING TASK

WRITE A FIRST DRAFT

1 🔒 Ask learners to choose two malls from Table 7.1 in the Critical thinking section to write a comparison of.

2 🔒 Focus on the prompts (1–8). Learners use the prompts to write sentences comparing the two malls they have chosen. You could support learners by eliciting/modelling examples for the more complex sentences and putting these on the board. Remind them to use … *is the same as … / The two malls have the same number of …* if the two malls have the same features. Remind learners to join their comparison sentences using *but*.

EDIT

3 and 4 🔒 Focus on the task checklist. Go through the checklist to make sure learners know what to check. Then ask learners to edit their work, using the checklist to help them. You can ask learners to produce a final draft of their work before handing it in. If not, collect in their edited first draft to mark and correct. If the writing task has produced some common errors, highlight these in later lessons, using the model answer to give examples.

Answers

See page 137 for a model answer.

OBJECTIVES REVIEW

See Introduction, page 9, for ideas about using the Objectives Review with your learners.

WORDLIST

See Introduction, page 9, for ideas about how to make the most of the Wordlist with your learners.

REVIEW TEST

See page 117 for the photocopiable Review Test for this unit and page 94, for ideas about when and how to administer the Review Test.

RESEARCH PROJECT

Create an interactive map for new learners.

Divide the class into teams ask them to think about an orientation guide for new learners. Ask each team to draw or create a map of their learning environment or campus and to think of descriptions for each one of the locations they draw.

Using an online application, learners can scan or take a photo of their map and populate it with descriptions and photos. There can then be a competition for the best map to be distributed to new learners.

8 FOOD AND CULTURE

Learning objectives

Go through the learning objectives with the class to make sure everyone understands what they can expect to achieve in this unit. Point out that learners will have a chance to review these objectives again at the end of the unit.

UNLOCK YOUR KNOWLEDGE

Lead-in

👥 Tell the class what you had for breakfast today, e.g. *I had tea, toast, jam and a banana.* Ask: *What did you have for breakfast today?* Give learners one minute to tell their partners. For feedback, ask one or two pairs to tell the class.

Optional activity

👤 Choose ten letters of the alphabet. Say each letter and ask learners to write down a food and/or a drink (more than one, if they can) beginning with that letter, e.g. *b* (*bread, butter*), *c* (*cake, coffee*), *f* (*fruit, fish*), *m* (*milk, meat*), *p* (*pizza, potato*), *s* (*sandwich, sugar*), *t* (*tea, tomato*), etc. The learner with the most food or drink words at the end is the winner.

1 👥 Focus on the questions. You could give your own answers first as an example. Revise the meaning of *traditional* if necessary. Learners ask and answer the questions in pairs. At the end, ask one or two learners to share their answers with the class.

For stronger learners / fast finishers, write further discussion questions on the board: *Do people cook your favourite food at home? Do you buy it in the street/at a restaurant, etc.? Can you cook it? Is it difficult to cook? What's in it? (meat, rice, fish, vegetables?)*

WATCH AND LISTEN

Optional activity

Focus on the video stills at the top of the page and ask learners to say what they can see.

PREPARING TO WATCH

UNDERSTANDING KEY VOCABULARY

1 👤 Ask learners to match the words to the definitions, using the photographs and glossary on page 199 to help them. Check answers with the class. Learners should remember *chef* and *restaurant* from Unit 6.

> **Answers**
> 1 d 2 c 3 b 4 a

2 👤 Ask learners to complete the sentences with the words from Exercise 1. Check answers with the class. Ask: *Is there a market in your town/city? Do you buy food there?*

> **Answers**
> 1 chef 2 chocolate 3 restaurant 4 market

WHILE WATCHING

UNDERSTANDING MAIN IDEAS

3 ▶️👤 Ask learners if they know anything about Mexico. Focus on the true/false statements and pre-teach the meaning of *sauce*. Play the video. Learners write (T) or (F) next to each statement. Check answers with the class.

> **Answers**
> 1 T
> 2 T
> 3 F She is opening a new restaurant.
> 4 F He is helping Martha with the design of her new restaurant.
> 5 F *Mole* is a famous Mexican sauce.
> 6 T

LISTENING FOR KEY INFORMATION

4 ▶️👤 Play the video again. Learners answer the questions. Play the video again if necessary. Check answers with the class.

Answers

1 Between the Gulf of Mexico, the Pacific and the Caribbean Sea
2 beautiful beaches and old buildings
3 Mexico City
4 food

Video script

Mexico is famous for its beautiful beaches and old buildings. The country is between the Gulf of Mexico, the Pacific and the Caribbean Sea. It is a beautiful place.

Mexico has many big cities. The biggest is Mexico City.

Food is very important to the people of Mexico. The first chocolate came from Mexico.

Martha Ortiz lives in Mexico City. She is a chef. Martha is opening a new restaurant. There is lots of work to do. Victor Zapatero is helping Martha with the design of the restaurant.

Martha is going to a market. She needs to buy food for the first night of the restaurant. She finds what she wants.

She enjoys making the food. Martha is making a famous Mexican sauce. It is called *mole*. Martha uses chocolate to make *mole*.

Everything is ready. Martha can now enjoy the first night of her new restaurant.

5 ▶ 👤 Focus on the multiple-choice questions. Learners watch and circle the correct options. Check answers with the class. Ask: *Have you eaten Mexican food? Do you like it?*

Answers

1 a   2 c   3 b

Background note

Mexican food is a mixture of different cooking traditions. It is influenced by indigenous Central American cooking. This is seen in important native food items such as corn, beans and chilli peppers. Mexican food is also influenced by European and particularly Spanish cooking, following the Spanish conquest of the Aztec Empire.

DISCUSSION

6 👥 Learners ask and answer the questions in pairs. Ask one or two pairs to tell the class what they found out about their partner. Pay particular attention to how they use any vocabulary from the lesson and any issues with meaning or pronunciation.

READING 1

PREPARING TO READ

PREVIEWING

1 👤 As revision, elicit the kinds of things learners should look at while previewing a text. Focus on the three sentences and elicit/teach the meanings of *international* and *Asian*. Allow a short time limit of 10–20 seconds for learners to preview the texts and circle the correct options. Check answers with the class. Ask learners to explain why they chose the options they did, e.g. 1 *The design and print in the three texts are the same.* 2 *The photographs show different nationalities.* 3 *The heading contains the word 'world' not Asia / The text refers to British tea.*

Answers

1 the same book   2 different   3 international

UNDERSTANDING KEY VOCABULARY

2 👤 Focus on the wordbox and the gapped sentences. Learners complete the sentences with the words from the box, using a dictionary to help them. Check answers with the class and model and drill pronunciation of any difficult words, e.g. *guest* /gest/, *taste* /teɪst/, *pull* /pʊl/, *pour* /pɔː/, *kettle* /ˈketl/ and *prepare* /prɪˈpeə/.

Answers

1 tastes   2 leaves   3 pour   4 prepare
5 pull   6 kettle   7 guests

WHILE READING

SKIMMING

3 👤 Focus on the *Skimming* box. Explain that we can skim a text quickly to find the main topic and idea of a text. We do not read every word, but pick out important words, such as nouns, verbs, adjectives and question words. Focus on the statements (1–4). Ask learners to read only the blue words in the texts and decide if the statements are true or false. Check answers with the class. Elicit correct versions of the false sentences.

Answers

1 F The texts are only about tea. 2 T
3 F There are many kinds of tea. 4 T

SCANNING TO FIND INFORMATION

4 👤 Focus on the first gapped sentence and ask learners which word(s) they will scan the texts for (*teh tarik*). Point out that they need the names of countries to fill the gaps and that they should read around the scanned-for words when they have located them to find the answer. Set a time limit (up to three minutes) for the whole exercise to ensure learners scan read. Check answers with the class.

Answers

1 Malaysia (Kuala Lumpur is the capital city.)
2 Russia
3 Japan
4 Russia
5 Turkey
6 Malaysia

DISCUSSION

5 👥 Before this pairwork, get an able learner to ask you the questions and give your answers as examples. Pairs ask and answer the questions. For feedback, ask one or two pairs to tell the class their partner's answers. Ask stronger learners to describe how they make tea to revise some of the vocabulary from this lesson, e.g. *prepare, tea leaves, kettle, taste, pour.*

Optional activity

Conduct a quick class survey on learners' favourite drinks, e.g. *Do you prefer hot or cold drinks? What is your favourite cold drink?* Record the results on the board and revise *more than* by eliciting sentences such as *Coffee is more popular than tea,* etc.

READING 2

PREPARING TO READ

PREVIEWING

1 👤 Focus on sentences 1 and 2. Allow a short time limit of 10 seconds for learners to quickly preview the text and photographs and circle the correct words. Check answers with the class.

Answers

1 students 2 kinds of food

UNDERSTANDING KEY VOCABULARY

2 👤 Ask learners to match the words in the box to the photographs using the glossary on page 199 to help them. Check answers with the class. Model and drill pronunciation, e.g. *pineapple* /ˈpaɪnæpl/, *mushroom* /ˈmʌʃruːm/ and *cabbage* /ˈkæbɪdʒ/.

Answers

1 pineapple 2 mushroom 3 cabbage 4 rice

3 👤 Focus on the gapped sentences. Check learners understand *waiter* /ˈweɪtə/ (= a person who works in a restaurant and brings the food to customers at their tables) and elicit the first answer as an example. Learners use the glossary on page 199 to help them complete the remaining sentences. If your learners are less able, you could do the whole exercise as a class. Check answers with the class and model and drill pronunciation of *cuisine* /kwɪˈziːn/. Make sure learners understand the differences between the three sentences with *serve* (see the answer key). Provide personalized practice of the words and phrases by eliciting examples of local/national dishes learners know. Ask them what they are served with (e.g. rice, potatoes) or served in (e.g. on a plate/in a bowl).

Answers

1 serves (gives out)
2 is served with (+ food items usually eaten together)
3 is served in (+ the container used)
4 dish
5 cuisine

Language note

Cuisine (from French) means a style of cooking, e.g. *Italian cuisine, French cuisine*; a *dish* is one part of a meal, e.g. *steak frites, lasagne.*

WHILE READING

SCANNING TO FIND INFORMATION

4 👤 Focus on the statements. Make sure learners understand *alphabetical order*. Learners scan the text and mark the statements true or

false. Set a time limit (up to two minutes) to ensure learners scan rather than read closely. Check answers with the class and elicit correct versions of the false statements. Ask: *Have you eaten any of these dishes? Would you like to eat any of the other dishes?*

Answers
1 T
2 F *Sharwarma* is a savoury meat dish.
3 F *Amok trey* is a Cambodian dish.
4 T
5 F Pineapple is popular in Cambodian cuisine.
6 T
7 F Cambodian food is served with mushrooms and cabbage.

Background note
The Arab world is made up of the Arabic-speaking countries of North Africa and western Asia.

Cambodia, officially known as the Kingdom of Cambodia, is in southeast Asia. The capital city is Phnom Penh, the official language is Khmer and the population is approximately 14.3 million.

Australia, officially the Commonwealth of Australia, is the sixth largest country in the world by area with 7.7 million square kilometres (2.9 million square miles). Its capital is Canberra, its largest city is Sydney and its population is approximately 22.6 million.

READING FOR DETAIL

5 Focus on the questions. Learners can read the whole text closely this time in order to answer the questions. However, as an alternative to reading the whole text closely and then answering the questions, you could ask learners to use key words in the questions to scan for the relevant parts of the text and then read just those sections closely. Check answers with the class. Discuss the answer to question 3 briefly as learners need to find a synonym for *healthy* (= *good for you*).

Answers
1 Middle Eastern countries and Saudi Arabia
2 *Sharwarma* and kangaroo burgers
3 crocodile and kangaroo
4 Arab and Cambodian
5 Australian and Cambodian

DISCUSSION

6 Get a learner to ask you the questions first as a model. Learners then discuss the questions in pairs. For feedback, ask one or

two pairs to report their partner's answers to the class. Provide extension questions for fast finishers / more able learners, e.g.: *Do you like cuisine from other countries? Why / Why not? What is your favourite foreign cuisine? How often do you eat it?*

LANGUAGE DEVELOPMENT

VOCABULARY FOR FOOD AND DRINK

1 Focus on the photographs. Elicit any food words learners already know, then ask them to write the words in the box under the correct photographs, using a dictionary to help them. Check answers with the class. Model and drill pronunciation of any difficult words, e.g. *date* /deɪt/, *onion* /'ʌnjən/, *chillis* /'tʃɪliz/, *spice* /spaɪs/, *almond* /'ɑːmənd/ and *yoghurt* /'jɒgət/. Ask: *Which of these do you like / don't you like?*

Answers
1 milk 2 dates 3 butter 4 chillis 5 potatoes 6 honey 7 spices 8 almonds 9 water 10 onion 11 yoghurt 12 coconut

Countable and uncountable nouns

Focus on the *Countable and uncountable nouns* explanation box. Revise singular and plural if necessary and the use of a singular verb after a singular noun / a plural verb after a plural noun.

Use simple sketches on the board to show the differences between countable items, i.e. we can count them (e.g. three carrots, four apples) and uncountable items that we can't count (e.g. spaghetti, rice, water).

Elicit more example sentences containing countable and uncountable food words from learners and write them on the board. Ask learners to make sure the nouns and verbs agree.

Language note
Countable nouns can have the word *a/an* in front of them or they can be used in the plural. Uncountable nouns are not used with *a/an* or in the plural. Some nouns can be countable and uncountable with slightly different meanings (e.g. *coffee* = dark brown powder made from coffee beans, *a coffee* = a cup of coffee). *Fish* is considered uncountable in this unit because it is a food item.

Optional activity

Look at the foods in the photographs on page 149 and ask learners which are countable and which uncountable. Alternatively, write food words on the board and ask learners to decide if they are countable or uncountable, e.g. (U) *bread, cheese, pasta, water*; (C) *eggs, dates, almonds, onions*.

2 👤 Focus on the sentences and elicit the first answer as an example. Learners put a tick next to the remaining correct sentences and a cross next to the incorrect ones. Check answers with the class.

> **Answers**
>
> Correct: 2, 4, 5, 6, 7, 10, 11
> Incorrect: 1, 3, 8, 9, 12

3 👤 Ask learners to correct the mistakes in Exercise 2. Elicit the first answer as an example. Check answers with the class. Make sure learners correct both the plural nouns and the plural verbs here. Check understanding of *soup* /suːp/ (= a usually hot liquid food made from vegetables, meat or fish) and ask if it is countable or uncountable (uncountable).

> **Answers**
>
> 1 <u>Honey is</u> sweet.
> 3 <u>Milk is</u> good for children.
> 8 <u>Butter is</u> served with bread.
> 9 <u>Yoghurt is</u> served with many Middle Eastern dishes.
> 12 <u>Water is</u> served in a glass.

CRITICAL THINKING

Go through the instructions with the class and focus on the writing task. Explain that the following sections of the unit will help them to prepare to write descriptive sentences about food in their country for a student website.

UNDERSTAND

Brainstorming

Focus on the *Brainstorming* box. Explain that brainstorming means discussing a topic with a group of people, either to think of new ideas or to prepare for a project or some writing. The group can make a note of all the relevant ideas and words connected to the topic.

1 Focus on the brainstorming notes and elicit answers to the questions (1–3) as a whole class. Elicit the meanings of any new words or explain them to the class.

> **Answers**
>
> 1 food (French) / a meal
> 2 countable (noun)
> 3 uncountable (noun)

APPLY

2 👤 Ask learners to read the gapped text about French cuisine. Then elicit the correct words from the notes in Exercise 1 to fill the first gap. Learners complete the rest of the text with the words from the notes. Check answers with the class. Ask: *Do you know either of these dishes? Do you like them? Would you like to eat them?*

> **Answers**
>
> 1 steak frites 2 crème brûlée 3 chips 4 butter
> 5 pepper 6 cream

3 👥 Tell learners that they are going to practise brainstorming themselves. Put them into small groups of three or four. First, ask them to choose two popular dishes from their country. Then ask them to brainstorm the food (= the ingredients) used to make these dishes, writing notes similar to those in the brainstorming notes for Exercise 1. Make sure the learners all write notes as they will need these for the Writing task later in the unit. Learners may want to list ingredients that are difficult to translate or that do not have an English name; suggest learners use another similar item or a general term, e.g. *a herb*, *spices*.

> **Answers**
>
> Answers will vary.

4 👥 Ask learners to use their dictionaries to decide which nouns in their brainstorming notes are countable and which are uncountable. Ask them to add this information to their notes.

> **Language note**
>
> Some dictionaries use U rather than UC to mean *uncountable*.

WRITING

GRAMMAR FOR WRITING

Subject–Verb agreement

Focus on the Subject–Verb agreement explanation box. Highlight the matching of singular noun with singular verb / plural noun with plural verb, i.e. they 'agree'. Point out the irregular plural children here also. Revise the use of a singular verb with an uncountable noun and elicit examples, e.g. Rice is nice, Honey is sweet, etc.

Optional activity

Ask learners to write gapped sentences and give them to a partner to complete with the correct verb forms, e.g. *A kangaroo burger … (is) good for you, Vegetables … (are) healthy.*

---

1 👤 Focus on the sentences (1–6) and elicit the correct option for the first question. Learners circle the remaining correct verb forms. Check answers with the class.

> **Answers**
> 1 prepare 2 uses 3 is 4 is 5 is 6 are

2 👤👥 Focus on the sentences and elicit or pre-teach the meanings of *hummus* (UC) and *hamburger* (C). Ask: *Do you think they are countable or uncountable?* Elicit the first answer from the class as an example. Learners mark the remaining sentences as correct or incorrect, then check their answers in pairs. Check answers with the class.

> **Answers**
> Correct: 2, 5
> Incorrect: 1, 3, 4, 6

3 👤 Elicit the correct version of sentence 1 in Exercise 2 as an example. Learners correct the remaining incorrect sentences. Note that here they only have to change the verbs. Check answers with the class.

> **Answers**
> 1 Egyptian <u>restaurants serve</u> falafel with cucumber sauce.
> 3 Nigerian <u>chefs prepare</u> pepper soup with fish or meat.
> 4 <u>Hamburgers are</u> served in bread.
> 6 French onion <u>soup is</u> delicious.

Determiners: *A, An* and *Some*

Focus on the *Determiners: a, an and some* explanation box. Go through the examples asking learners if the nouns are singular or plural countable nouns or if they are uncountable nouns. Ask: *Is dish countable or uncountable?* (countable). *Why is it **a** and not **an**?* (because it comes before a consonant sound: *famous*). *Why can't we say **a** honey?* (because *honey* is uncountable).

Language note

A determiner is a word used before a noun to show which noun you are talking about. Determiners include articles (*a/an* and *the*) and words like *some, this, his,* etc. We use the articles *a/an* in front of a singular countable noun when we talk about something/someone for the first time; we use *the* in front of a singular or plural noun when we mention something/someone that has already been mentioned or if everyone knows which thing(s)/people we are talking about.

Some is a determiner and a quantifier; it tells us how many or how much of something (countable or uncountable) there is.

The zero article (neither *a/an* nor *the*) is used before uncountable nouns and before countable plural nouns when we talk generally about people or things rather than about specific people or things, e.g. *English people drink tea (not the tea) with milk (not the milk); Chefs (= chefs in general) prepare the dish with some lemons.*

---

4 👥 Focus on sentences (1–8) and elicit the correction for the first underlined mistake. Learners can work in pairs to correct the remaining mistakes, or, as it is quite difficult, you may prefer to do this exercise together with the whole class. Learners may ask why *some* is not used in front of *crocodile meat* in question 6 or why *some* may be omitted in questions 2 and 5, so explain the use of the zero article with uncountable nouns when talking about things in general/making general statements (see Language note).

> **Answers**
> 1 At <u>some Arab restaurants</u>, you can find delicious beef dishes.
> 2 The curry is served with ~~a~~ <u>rice/some rice</u>.
> 3 <u>Some famous dishes</u> in New Orleans <u>are</u> *jambalaya* and *gumbo*.
> 4 French chefs add <u>an apple</u> to this dish.
> 5 Emirati chefs prepare *harees* with ~~a~~ (some) <u>meat</u> or ~~a~~ (some) <u>chicken</u>.
> 6 <u>Australians</u> like eating ~~a~~ <u>crocodile meat</u>.
> 7 There are <u>some carrots</u> in Korean *kim chee*.
> 8 <u>A popular dish</u> in Lagos is pepper soup.

ACADEMIC WRITING SKILLS

SPELLING

1 👤👥 Focus on the sentences containing adjectives with missing vowels. Elicit the correct vowels to complete the first adjective. Tell learners they can find the full forms of all these adjectives in the unit. Learners complete the remaining adjectives before checking their answers in pairs. Check answers with the class.

> ### Answers
> 1 sweet 2 savoury 3 delicious 4 spicy
> 5 healthy 6 tasty

Optional activity

Write foods from this unit on the board and get learners to make their own like/dislike sentences about them using the adjectives from this exercise, e.g. *I like chillis; they are very tasty. I don't like curry; it's very spicy.*

WRITING TASK

WRITE A FIRST DRAFT

1 👤 Ask learners to look at the brainstorming notes they wrote for two dishes from their country for Exercise 3 in the Critical thinking section.

2 👤 Ask learners to read the gapped text and complete it with correct information about their two dishes. If appropriate to your class, you could model this by asking learners to look back at the Reading 2 text and working together to complete the gapped paragraph for Cambodian cuisine on the board.

> *Cambodian* cuisine At a *Cambodian* restaurant, you find many different kinds of *fruit. Rice dishes* are very popular. *Cambodian* cuisine is also famous for *fish dishes.*

3 👤 Ask learners to write further sentences about their dishes using their brainstorming notes.

EDIT

4 and 5 👤 Focus on the task checklist. Go through the checklist to make sure learners know what to check. Then ask learners to edit their work, using the checklist to help them. You can ask learners to produce a final draft of their work before handing it in. If not, collect in their edited first draft to mark and correct. If the writing task has produced some common errors, highlight these in later lessons, using the model answer to give examples.

> ### Answers
> See page 138 for a model answer.

OBJECTIVES REVIEW

See Introduction, page 9, for ideas about using the Objectives Review with your learners.

WORDLIST

See Introduction, page 9, for ideas about how to make the most of the Wordlist with your learners.

REVIEW TEST

See page 120 for the photocopiable Review Test for this unit and page 94, for ideas about when and how to administer the Review Test.

RESEARCH PROJECT

Write your own recipe book and sell it for charity.

After dividing the class into teams, tell the learners that they are going to write a recipe book which can be organized into soups, appetizers, main courses and deserts. Tell them that they should include recipes which have ingredients that are easy to obtain locally. They could even give the book a theme. The learners can take photographs of their own cooking.

Learners will publish the recipes as an eBook so they will need to think about the best way to do this online.

---

9 THE ANIMAL KINGDOM

Learning objectives

Go through the learning objectives with the class to make sure everyone understands what they can expect to achieve in this unit. Point out that learners will have a chance to review these objectives again at the end of the unit.

UNLOCK YOUR KNOWLEDGE

Lead-in

Pre-teach *wild* (= animals living in natural conditions, not kept in a house or on a farm) and elicit the meaning of *wildlife* (= animals and plants that grow independently of people, usually in natural conditions). Ask: *How many wild animals do you know in English?* and get learners to write down as many as they can in one minute, e.g. *lion, tiger, elephant, rhino, giraffe, leopard, hippopotamus, crocodile.* Find out who listed the most animals and give an extra mark to anyone who has an animal that no one else has.

Focus on the wordbox and the gapped sentences and elicit the first answer as an example. Ask learners to complete the sentences. Check answers with the class. Model and drill pronunciation of any difficult words, e.g. *reptile* /ˈreptaɪl/, *mammal* /ˈmæml/ and *penguin* /ˈpeŋgwɪn/. You could check that learners have understood the words in bold by eliciting other kinds of animals for each group:

  Reptile: *gecko, snake, crocodile, turtle*
  Insect: *fly, beetle, mosquito*
  Mammal: *human, elephant, dolphin*
  Bird: *eagle, owl*

Answers

1 snake 2 bee 3 bear 4 penguin

Optional activity

Show pictures of other animals and ask learners to decide which animal group they belong to.

WATCH AND LISTEN

PREPARING TO WATCH

USING YOUR KNOWLEDGE TO PREDICT CONTENT

1 Before they watch the video, use a map to check that learners know where South Africa is. Ask: *Is it hot or cold in South Africa? What animals do you think you will see in the video?* Working in small groups, learners discuss and write a list of three animals they think they will see. The video stills will also give them some clues here. Ask one or two groups to report back to the class. Model and drill pronunciation of any difficult words, e.g. *rhino* /ˈraɪnəʊ/, *giraffe* /dʒɪˈrɑːf/, *springbok* /ˈsprɪŋbɒk/, *zebra* /ˈzebrə/ (US pronunciation /ˈziːbrə/).

Background note

South Africa, officially the Republic of South Africa, is located at the southern end of the African continent. It covers an area of 1.22 million square kilometres (470,693 square miles) and it has a population of approximately 50.5 million. It has three capitals, Pretoria (executive capital), Cape Town (legislative capital) and Bloemfontein (judicial capital) but the largest city is Johannesburg. It has 11 official languages including English, Afrikaans, Sesotho, Setswana, Xhosa and Zulu.

Possible answers

penguin, springbok, lion, zebra, giraffe, elephant, rhino(ceros), hippo(potamus) (not tigers, which are only found in the wild in Asia)

2 Play the video with no sound. Ask: *What animals can you see? How many animals on your list were in the video? Did anything surprise you?*

Answers

Animals in the video: penguin, springbok, lion, zebra, elephant, giraffe, rhino

UNDERSTANDING KEY VOCABULARY

3 👤 Ask learners to check the meanings of the words in the box using a dictionary to help them.

4 👤 Focus on the definitions and check learners understand them. Revise the meaning of *typical* and contrast it with *unusual* by eliciting typical/unusual types of hobbies or pets. Learners write the words from the box in Exercise 3 in the gaps. Check answers with the class. Model and drill the pronunciation of any difficult words, e.g. *species* /'spiːʃiːʒ/, *powerful* /'paʊəfl/, *diversity* /daɪ'vɜːsɪtɪ/ and *savannah* /sə'vænə/.

> **Answers**
>
> 1 species 2 powerful 3 unusual 4 diversity 5 grass
> 6 savannah

WHILE WATCHING

LISTENING FOR KEY INFORMATION

5 ▶️👤 Focus on the table. Elicit possible adjectives for each animal from learners before they watch the video again, e.g.:

> *Springboks are … fast.*
> *Lions are … dangerous.*
> *Elephants are … big.*
> *Rhinos are … strong.*
> *Penguins are … small.*

Play the video again, this time with the sound. Learners write the adjectives they hear for each animal in column A. You could stop the video at a suitable point and elicit one or two examples first. Point out that there could be more than one adjective for each animal and learners may have to write more than one word. Check answers with the class. Note that some of the adjectives in the video are superlative forms which are taught explicitly in the *Grammar for writing* section later in the unit.

> **Answers**
>
> See Exercise 6.

6 ▶️👤 Focus on column B of the table in Exercise 5. Play the video again. Learners write any numbers they hear about rhinos and penguins in column B. Check answers with the class.

Answers

animals	A adjectives	B numbers
springboks	popular fast tough	
lions and elephants	the most popular interesting	
rhinos	interesting one of the most powerful not the fastest one of the most dangerous	2,000 40
penguins	the most unusual not afraid (of people) popular	4,000

7 👤 Focus on the phrases. Learners use the numbers they wrote in column B to fill the gaps. Check answers with the class. Check understanding and pronunciation of *weight* /weɪt/. Revise the use of acronyms for *kg* (= *kilogram*) /'kɪləgræm/ and *kph* (= *kilometres per hour*) /ˌkeɪpiː'eɪtʃ/ UK /'kɪləˌmiːtə/ US /kɪ'lɑːmətə/.

> **Answers**
>
> a 4,000 b 40 c 2,000

> **VIDEO SCRIPT**
>
> Morning. South Africa. This is a land of diversity. The savannah is the home of about 300 species of wildlife.
>
> These zebras travel in groups called herds. They only stop to drink water or eat grass.
>
> And these are springboks. They are popular in South Africa. Springboks are fast and tough.
>
> Many tourists come to South Africa from other countries. They come to see the wildlife. Lions and elephants are the most popular animals. But there are many other interesting animals in South Africa.
>
> Here is one of them. The rhino is one of the most powerful animals in the world. This rhino is almost 2,000 kilograms. But he can run at 40 kilometres per hour. It is not the fastest animal in the world. But it can be one of the most dangerous.
>
> South Africa also has a diverse sea life. There are more than 11,000 species of plants and animals in or near South Africa's oceans.
>
> Penguins are perhaps the most unusual animals you can see in South Africa. Four thousand penguins live on Boulders Beach near Cape Town. They are not afraid of people! Penguins are very popular with the tourists in South Africa.
>
> South Africa is a land of diversity.

DISCUSSION

8 👥 Learners ask and answer the questions in pairs. For feedback, ask one or two pairs to report back to the class. You could use this opportunity to revise *more popular than* by eliciting, e.g. *Horses are more popular than dogs in my country.* Find out if any learners have unusual pets (or pets which could be considered wild animals), e.g. snakes, mice, etc.

READING 1

PREPARING TO READ

PREVIEWING

1 👤 Focus on the sentences. Ask learners to preview the text and the photographs as quickly as possible and circle the correct words. Check answers with the class.

> **Answers**
> 1 university students 2 unusual

> **Background note**
>
> The text is from an introduction to an academic textbook. Several features show that this is a book for university students, including the scientific title, the university publishing house and the inclusion of Latin names in the text. Latin is used for scientific classification because Latin was a lingua franca and the language of learning in Europe during the Renaissance. Although the common name of a plant or animal will differ between (and even within) languages, the Latin name is the universally recognized scientific term.

UNDERSTANDING KEY VOCABULARY

2 👤 Focus on the sentences (1–7). Learners write the words from the box in the gaps, using the glossary on page 200 to help them. Check answers with the class. (If learners need more help, draw two hearts on the board for *romantic*; a sketch of a chicken laying eggs for *lay eggs*. You could draw and measure a line on the board to show … *long*.) Model and drill pronunciation of any difficult words, e.g. *romantic* /rəʊ'mæntɪk/, *weigh* /weɪ/ and *variety* /və'raɪəti/. You could elicit further sentences using the words to check learners' understanding. The phrase *animal kingdom* is used in the reading text to mean 'all the

animals that exist in the world' (the normal sense of *kingdom* [= the country or area ruled by a king or queen as in *United Kingdom*] is not used in the text).

> **Answers**
> 1 romantic 2 kingdom 3 lays eggs 4 weighs
> 5 strange 6 long 7 variety

WHILE READING

READING FOR MAIN IDEAS

Focus on the *Reading for the main ideas* box. Explain that when we write a long text, we organize all our ideas into paragraphs. Usually, one paragraph contains one main idea. The main idea is usually introduced or summed up in the topic sentence, which is usually the first or second sentence in the paragraph. The other sentences add details and supporting information.

3 👤 Focus on the instructions and the highlighted sentences in the reading text. Ask: *How many paragraphs are there in Reading 1?* (five). Focus on the options (a–c) and ask learners to read the topic sentences and circle the correct option. Set a time limit of 40 seconds to ensure learners only read the topic sentences. Check the answer with the class. Talk about why (c) is the correct answer and elicit key words in the highlighted sentences that helped learners choose this answer (*animal kingdom, Australia, New Zealand, Asia = around the world; the strangest, strange = unusual*).

> **Answer**
> c

READING FOR DETAIL

4 👤👥 Focus on the questions (1–4). Learners read the text again and answer them. You could ask learners to read the whole text through and then answer the comprehension questions. Alternatively, ask them to look for key words in the questions and then scan for these in the text, reading carefully around these key words to answer the questions. The second alternative is the way effective readers interact with texts. Learners check their answers in pairs. Check answers with the class. Question 4 (*How big is the bumblebee bat?*) could refer to the length of the bumblebee bat or its weight or both, so it is best to answer this question with both its size and its weight. You could also ask: *Which animals usually lay eggs? Why do you think a bumblebee bat is called this?*

> ### Answers
>
> 1 It is a bird but it cannot fly.
> 2 Male and female kiwis live together for 30 years.
> 3 It lays eggs; mammals usually have live babies.
> 4 It is 2.5 centimetres long and it weighs 3 grams.

Optional discussion

👥 Put learners in pairs to discuss the questions below. Ask one or two pairs to report back to the class. Learners could also use the Internet to research a couple of animals from their country and make a labelled poster for display in the classroom.

Have you seen any of the animals in the reading text? Where? (TV/zoos?)
What wild animals do you have in your country?
Are there any strange/unusual animals in your country?
Do you like watching wildlife films?
Do you like visiting zoos/wildlife parks? Why / Why not?
What animals would you like to see in the wild? (in the wild = in their natural living area)

READING 2

PREPARING TO READ

UNDERSTANDING KEY VOCABULARY

1 🧍 Focus on the sentence halves. Elicit the first complete sentence as an example. Learners read and match the remaining halves, using the glossary on page 200 to check the words in bold. Check answers with the class and show pictures of the animals from the Internet if necessary. Model and drill the pronunciation of any difficult words, e.g. *prey* /preɪ/ and *squid* /ʃkwɪd/.

> ### Answers
>
> 1 d 2 h 3 a 4 f 5 g 6 b 7 c 8 e

USING YOUR KNOWLEDGE

2 Ask learners to close their books and write 'The World's Fastest Hunters' on the board. Ask: *Which animals are the world's fastest hunters?* Elicit and discuss ideas from the whole class and write learners' suggestions on the board.

> ### Possible answers
>
> cheetahs, leopards, sharks, humans

Optional activity

Discuss learners' suggestions for Exercise 2 and elicit which ones they think are faster/slower using comparative adjectives, e.g. *The … is faster than … / slower than …* . List the animals in the order the class agree on, from fastest to slowest.

WHILE READING

SKIMMING

3 🧍 Revise the skimming technique and ask learners which types of words they will look for in the reading text (nouns, verbs, adjectives, question words). Ask learners to skim the texts to find which three animals are the fastest hunters. Set a time limit of one or two minutes. Check answers with the class.

> ### Answers
>
> On land: cheetahs
> In the sea: sailfish
> In the air: peregrine falcons

SCANNING TO FIND INFORMATION

4 🧍👥 Focus on the table and the row headings to make sure learners understand them. Check: *lifespan* /ˈlaɪfspæn/ (= the length of time for which a person or animal lives); *habitat* /ˈhæbɪtæt/ (= the place, i.e. air, water, land, where an animal or plant usually lives); *common name* (= the everyday name for animals, not the scientific name).

Elicit examples of the things (i.e. numbers, names of countries/continents/oceans, animal nouns) learners will be looking for in the texts for each of the categories. Demonstrate the activity by completing the first gap with the class. You may need to do more than one example together, especially with weaker classes. Remind learners to write notes in the table rather than full sentences and point out that they do not need to include the units of measurement (e.g. *cm*) as these are already given in the row headings. Demonstrate the use of a dash to show ranges of measurements, e.g. *between 35 and 72 → 35–72*, by referring to examples in the reading text or writing some on the board; tell learners they can use this form in their notes. Learners complete the table, then check their answers in pairs. Check answers with the class.

Answers

scientific name	*Acinonyx jubatus*	*Istiophorus albicans* and *Istiophorus platypterus*	*Falco peregrinus*
common name	cheetah	sailfish	peregrine falcon
size (cm)	66–99 (high)	300 (long)	body 34–58 (long) wings 120 (long)
weight (kg)	35–72	90	1
lifespan (years)	12	4	15
speed (kph)	112	109	65–90 kph to 325 kph
habitat	East Africa / Iran	Atlantic, Indian and Pacific Oceans	cold and hot places / any country
prey	gazelles and zebras	other fish and squid	ducks and pigeons

UNDERSTANDING DISCOURSE

5 👤 Revise the meaning of *topic sentence* (= the sentence with the main idea or general introduction to a paragraph). Explain that in one paragraph in the three texts, the topic sentence is the second sentence. Ask learners to find it. Check the answer with the class. Discuss why it is the topic sentence (the first sentence of this paragraph is about sharks but the rest of the paragraph is about sailfish; the second sentence introduces this main idea). Compare with the first/topic sentences in the other texts.

Answers

The first paragraph in text B; the topic sentence is *The fastest swimmers are sailfish.*

⊙ LANGUAGE DEVELOPMENT

Can and *cannot*

Focus on the *Can and cannot* explanation box. Demonstrate how *can* and *not* join to make *cannot* (= one word). Learners should already know *can't* so explain that *cannot* is the usual form in formal written texts, such as the scientific texts in this unit. Contrast the different pronunciation of *can't* /kɑːnt/ and *cannot* /ˈkænɒt/. Provide personalized practice of *can/ cannot* (to describe ability) by asking questions and eliciting further examples, e.g. *Can you run? Can you run at 112 kph? Can you fly?* etc.

> **Language note**
>
> *Can* is a modal auxiliary verb. It has the same form for all persons/numbers and is followed by the bare infinitive, i.e. without *to*. *Can* is used: to express ability, e.g. *I **can** run*; to say what is or is not permitted, e.g. *You **can't** eat in the classrooms*; to describe the possibility of something being true, e.g. *The average wolf **can** weigh 60 kg.*

1 👤👥 Focus on the sentences (1–6). Correct the first sentence on the board with the whole class as an example. Learners correct the other underlined mistakes, then check their answers in pairs. Check answers with the whole class.

Answers

1 A wolf <u>can talk</u> to other wolves.
2 Wolves <u>can smell</u> blood.
3 The average wolf <u>can weigh</u> 60 kg.
4 Wolves <u>cannot to climb</u> trees.
5 Wolves <u>can to hunt</u> very big animals.
6 A wolf ~~no cannot live~~ in hot countries.

DESCRIBING FACTS ABOUT ANIMALS

2 👤👥 Focus on the gapped sentences (1–8). Ask more able classes to try to complete the sentences without looking at the wordbox first. Learners complete the sentences with the words from the box, then check their answers in pairs. Check answers with the class. Highlight the following verbs and prepositions: *run/fly **at*** + speed, *live **on*** (phrasal verb = *to eat*), *live **in*** + country, *live* *for* + time expression. Teach the use of *about* (= *approximately*).

Answers
1 at 2 weighs 3 on 4 long 5 high 6 in 7 for 8 at

Optional activity

Ask learners to find examples of the verbs + preposition patterns from this exercise in Reading 2:

at + speed, e.g. *Cheetahs can run at 112 kph; Sailfish can swim at 109 kph; Falcons usually fly at 65–90 kph*

for + time expression, e.g. *Cheetahs live for about 12 years; Sailfish live for about four years; Falcons live for about 15 years*

---

3   Ask learners to match the words (a–h) to the sentences (1–8) in Exercise 2. Elicit the first answer as an example. Check answers with the class. Elicit the meaning of *diet* (= the food and drink usually eaten by a person/animal) and model and drill pronunciation /ˈdaɪət/.

Answers
a 6 b 5 c 4 d 7 e 1 f 2 g 8 h 3

VOCABULARY FOR ANIMALS

4   Focus on the sentence halves and elicit the first match from the class, as an example. Learners match the remaining halves, using a dictionary to help them understand the words in bold. They may also need to look up *frog*. Show pictures from the Internet if necessary. Check answers with the class. Model and drill pronunciation of any difficult words, e.g. *nocturnal* /nɒkˈtɜːnəl/ and *amphibious* /æmˈfɪbɪəʃ/. You could elicit sentences about other *nocturnal/ amphibious/endangered/ venomous/harmless/deadly* animals from the class.

Answers
1 c 2 f 3 d 4 a 5 e 6 b

Language note

Note the common adjective endings: *-al* (*nocturnal*), *-ous* (*amphibious*), *-ed* (*endangered*), *-ly* (*deadly*) and *-less* (*harmless*). Another common adjective ending is *-ful* (*powerful*).

CRITICAL THINKING

Go through the instructions with the class and focus on the writing task. Explain that the following sections of the unit will help them to prepare to write a descriptive paragraph about an animal.

ANALYZE

1   Focus on Table 9.1. Learners can check any of the bold words they are not sure about in a dictionary. Ask questions to check understanding of the table, e.g. *What does a panda bear eat?* (bamboo) *How heavy is a polar bear?* (350 to 480 kg), etc. If you have Internet access in your classroom, show pictures of the different bears and ask learners to name them. Ask: *What does 'population' mean here?* (how many of each type of bear there are in the whole world) and explain that a low number in this section means a bear is endangered.

Language note

In the *population* row, *c.* is an abbreviation of the Latin word *circa* /ˈʃɜːkə/ (= *about, approximately*). This is often used in formal academic texts.

---

2   Focus on the questions and elicit the first answer from the whole class as an example. Pairs ask and answer the remaining questions. Monitor and give help where needed. Learners should be able to guess the meaning of *varied* in question 5 from *variety*. Check answers with the whole class. Ask: *Is any of the information surprising?*

Answers
1 the polar bear 2 the polar bear 3 the brown bear 4 the panda bear 5 the brown bear 6 the brown bear 7 the panda bear

3   Focus on the gapped text. Ask: *Which bear is the text about?* (the brown bear) *Which sentence is the topic sentence of the paragraph?* (the second sentence). Elicit the first missing word. Learners complete the rest of the text with the correct information from Table 9.1, then check their answers in pairs. Check answers with the class. Draw attention to the use of language from the Language development section in this text, e.g. *at* + speed, *live for* + time expression, *about*, *live on*, etc.

Answers

1 40 2 150 3 250 4 300 5 335 6 22 7 24
8 200,000 9 nuts 10 fish

WRITING

GRAMMAR FOR WRITING

Superlative adjectives

Focus on the *Superlative adjectives* explanation box and show how each of the patterns is formed using the board. If necessary, revise *syllable* from Unit 7 and elicit examples of one-, two- and three-syllable words first. Highlight the use of *the* before the superlative adjective. Remind learners about the doubling of consonants in some adjectives (e.g. *biggest, fattest,* etc.). Point out the prepositional phrase *in the* + noun or *on* + noun.

Language note

When a one-syllable adjective ends in a single vowel followed by a single consonant, we double the consonant when adding -*est*. We only add -*st* if an adjective already ends in -*e*, e.g. *strangest*. The final example in the explanation box shows a common error: learners often use instead of *biggest in the world/class/school.*

---

1 🧑 To demonstrate this activity, you could write the words and phrases in sentence 1 on separate large pieces of paper and stick them in jumbled order on the board. Ask a learner to rearrange them to make a sentence. Learners rearrange the remaining words to make sentences. Check answers with the class.

Answers

1 The fastest lizard in the world is the horned lizard. /
   The horned lizard is the fastest lizard in the world.
2 Sailfish are the fastest swimmers.
3 Peregrine falcons are the fastest birds on earth.
4 Polar bears are the biggest kind of bear.
5 The sea snake is the most venomous snake in the world. / The most venomous snake in the world is the sea snake.
6 The blue Morpho butterfly is the most beautiful butterfly in the world. / The most beautiful butterfly in the world is the blue Morpho butterfly.
7 The blue whale is the biggest animal in the world. / The biggest animal in the world is the blue whale.
8 The wolf spider is one of the deadliest spiders.

2 🧑🧑 Focus on the sentences (1–8) and ask learners whether the first sentence is correct

or incorrect. Learners read and put a tick or a cross next to the remaining sentences. Check answers with the class.

Answers

Correct sentences: 5, 6

3 🧑🧑 Elicit the correct version of sentence 1 in Exercise 2. Learners correct the remaining incorrect sentences from Exercise 2, then check their answers in pairs. Check answers with the class.

Answers

1 Cheetahs ~~in the world~~ are the fastest animal / animals ~~in the world~~.
2 Cats are some of the ~~more lazier~~ laziest animals in the world.
3 Kakopo parrots are the ~~more~~ most endangered kind of parrot.
4 Kiwis are the ugliest bird / birds in New Zealand.
7 Squid ~~in the sea~~ are one of the strangest animals in the sea.
8 The brown bear is the fastest kind of bear.

ACADEMIC WRITING SKILLS

SPELLING

1 🧑 Ask learners to put the jumbled letters in the correct order to make the names of animals. They can use the definitions to help them. Tell learners that all these animals can be found in the unit. Check answers with the class.

Answers

1 bat 2 bee 3 lion 4 bear 5 bird 6 wolf 7 shark 8 insect 9 falcon 10 spider

PUNCTUATION

2 🧑🧑 Learners add the missing capital letters and full stops to sentences (1–6). When they have finished, ask learners to swap their answers with a partner for correction. Check answers with the class.

Answers

1 Many venomous spiders live in Australia.
2 The most venomous Australian spider is also one of the smallest.
3 Redback spiders are only 1 cm long.
4 The deadliest spider in Australia is the redback spider.
5 Redback spiders live on small insects.
6 Female redback spiders live for two or three years.

WRITING TASK

PLAN

1. 👤 Ask learners to read the completed brown bear text in Exercise 3 of the Critical thinking section again. Tell them they will use this text as a model to help them write their own paragraph about a different bear.

2. 👤 Ask learners to choose the panda bear or the polar bear from Table 9.1 on page 168 to write a paragraph about. Ask them to read through the information in the table first before they make a decision.

3. 👤 Focus on the sentence prompts (1–8). Ask learners to write sentences about the bear they have chosen. They can use the models in the brown bear paragraph for help with forming sentences correctly. If you think your class would benefit, write one or two sentences together on the board first, e.g. *The scientific name for polar bears is Ursus maritimus.*

4. 👤 Ask learners to look at their sentences from Exercise 3 and the data in Table 9.1. They compare the bear they have just described with the other two bears by writing two sentences with comparative adjectives. If necessary, work together to write a model sentence on the board first, e.g. *A panda bear is smaller than a brown bear.* Using the same information, ask learners to write one or two sentences with superlative adjectives, e.g. *The polar bear is the biggest bear / Polar bears are the biggest bears.* It may help to elicit and write further comparative and superlative forms on the board, e.g.:

    lighter / the lightest
    heavier / the heaviest
    faster / the fastest
    slower / the slowest
    lives (for) longer / the longest

WRITE A FIRST DRAFT

5. 👤 Ask learners to put their sentences from Exercises 3 and 4 into a paragraph. Remind them about topic sentences and ask them to make a topic sentence the first sentence in their paragraph. You could suggest they use one of their superlative adjective sentences as the topic sentence / first sentence for their texts, e.g. *The panda bear is the most*

endangered bear. Give help and advice with this stage of the drafting. (Note that in the brown bear text the topic sentence is the second sentence.)

EDIT

6 and 7 👤 Focus on the task checklist. Go through the checklist to make sure learners know what to check. Then ask learners to edit their work, using the checklist to help them. You can ask learners to produce a final draft of their work before handing it in. If not, collect in their edited first draft to mark and correct. If the writing task has produced some common errors, highlight these in later lessons, using the model answer to give examples. Choose some good examples of writing from individual learners and ask them if you can share them with the class. These could be displayed on the walls of the classroom for the others to read, projected onto the board or photocopied and given out.

> **Answers**
> See page 139 for a model answer.

Optional activity

👥👥 Organize a class quiz about bears. First, make sure learners close their books. Put learners in teams (ideally with others who wrote about the same type of bear) and give each team a sheet of paper. Ask the questions below (allow learners a couple of minutes to discuss and then write down each answer before moving on to the next question). At the end, ask teams to swap sheets and mark another team's answers when you give the answers. The team with the most correct answers are the winners.

1) Which type of bear has the smallest population? (*Panda bear*)
2) What do polar bears live on? (*Seals*)
3) What do panda bears live on? (*Bamboo, mushrooms and fish*)
4) Which bear is the fastest? (*Brown bear*)
5) How fast can a polar bear run? (*35–40 kph*)
6) Which bear has the longest lifespan? (*Panda bear*)
7) Which bear is found in the USA, Canada, Europe and Asia? (*Brown bear*)
8) Which bear is the heaviest? (*Polar bear*)
9) Which bear is the smallest? (*Panda bear*)
10) What's the common name for *Ursus maritimus*? (*Polar bear*)

OBJECTIVES REVIEW

See Introduction, page 9, for ideas about using the Objectives Review with your learners.

WORDLIST

See Introduction, page 9, for ideas about how to make the most of the Wordlist with your learners.

REVIEW TEST

See page 123 for the photocopiable Review Test for this unit and page 94, for ideas about when and how to administer the Review Test.

RESEARCH PROJECT

Create your own Safari eBook and present it.

Explain to your class that they are going to research different species of local animals. They should find out whether some are endangered. Tell learners that they will be creating an ebook to inform the public of the different types. Each group could be assigned an animal group like reptiles, mammals, fish, birds or amphibians. They need to describe the class and information about each animal.

Learners can present these at a special animal event.

TRANSPORT

Learning objectives

Go through the learning objectives with the class to make sure everyone understands what they can expect to achieve in this unit. Point out that learners will have a chance to review these objectives again at the end of the unit.

UNLOCK YOUR KNOWLEDGE

Lead-in

👥 Elicit/pre-teach the meaning of *public transport* and ask: *What kinds of public transport are there in your town/city?* Give learners one minute to write down as many types of transport as they can. For feedback, ask one or two pairs to share their lists with the class, e.g. *buses, taxis, trains, coaches, trams, ferries, cable cars, rickshaws*, etc. Give a point for every correct item and give an extra point to a learner who has a correct item no one else has listed.

👥 Focus on the questions. Learners ask and answer in pairs. (Make sure learners use the correct prepositions in their answers to question 1, e.g. *by bus/train/car* but *on foot*; these are covered more explicitly later in this unit.) For feedback, ask one or two pairs to share their answers with the class, then open out the discussion of questions 3 and 4 to the whole class. You could use this opportunity to revise superlatives.

WATCH AND LISTEN

Optional activity

Focus on the video stills at the top of the page and ask learners to say what they can see. Use the first picture to pre-teach *bullet train*.

PREPARING TO WATCH

USING VISUALS TO PREDICT CONTENT

1 👤 Focus on the pie chart and map (Figures 10.1 and 10.2). Elicit the answer to the first question to make sure learners understand how to read

the pie chart. Learners answer the remaining questions (2–4), using a dictionary to check the words in bold. Note that *commute* (noun) in question 4 is also more commonly used as a verb. Check answers with the class.

Answers

1 metro
2 metro and bus
3 taxi and private car
4 830 km

Background note

Japan is an island country located in the Pacific Ocean in East Asia. The capital is Tokyo and the main language is Japanese. The four biggest islands are Honshu, Hokkaido, Kyushu and Shikoku. The population is approximately 127 million, the world's tenth largest population, and Japan has the world's third largest economy.

Background note

A metro is an underground railway system in some cities, e.g. Paris and Washington. In New York it is called the subway and in London it is called the underground or, informally, the tube.

WHILE WATCHING

LISTENING FOR KEY INFORMATION

2 ▶️ 👤 Focus on column A of the table. Play the video and ask learners to write the words for the different forms of transport that they both see and hear on the commentary in column A. Check answers with the class.

Answers

taxis   (urban) rail (system) / train   (bullet) train   plane

3 ▶️ 👤 Play the video again. Learners listen and write the numbers they hear in column B of the table in Exercise 2. Suggest that, where possible, learners write the numbers next to the relevant form of transport in column A. Check answers with the class.

Answers

13 million   50,000   8 million   300   10 million

4 👥 Focus on the statements (1–5). Put learners in pairs and ask them to decide if the statements are true or false, using their notes in the table in Exercise 2 to help them. Check answers with the class and elicit the correct versions of the false sentences.

Answers

1 F 13 million people live in Tokyo.
2 T
3 T
4 F Many people (more than 10 million) commute from Sapporo to Tokyo.
5 F 10 million passengers take the flight / fly between Tokyo and Sapporo every year.

Video script

Tokyo is one of the biggest cities in the world. Around 13 million people live here. Every day, millions more come to Tokyo to work. Transport in the city is very busy. How do people get to work? And how do they get around the city?

Tokyo has excellent public and private transport. There are over 50,000 taxis. And over 8 million passengers use the urban rail system every day.

The Shinkansen bullet train is a very fast way to get to Tokyo. The trains travel at up to 300 kilometres per hour. They are very efficient. They are almost never late.

Another popular way to commute to Tokyo is by plane. The flight between Tokyo and Sapporo, in North Japan, is the busiest in the world. More than 10 million passengers take this journey every year.

You can check in with your mobile phone.

A modern and efficient transport system is a very important part of everyday life in Tokyo.

MAKING INFERENCES

5 👥 Explain that when we make inferences /ˈɪnfərəntsɪs/, we deduce that something is true because of information we already have. Put learners in pairs and ask them to read the questions (1–3) and choose the best answers. Monitor learners' discussions here, helping if necessary. Check answers with the class and discuss learners' reasons for their answers. Ask: *Do you know anyone who commutes a long way to work?* and discuss the reasons for commuting long distances in general. Ask: *Would you like to visit Tokyo? Why / Why not?*

Answers

1 b 2 b 3 a

Optional activity

Revise comparatives by asking learners to compare their own town/city with Tokyo (or with Sapporo if your learners are from Tokyo). Elicit some adjectives to describe cities and write them on the board, e.g. *cheap, expensive, fast, slow, crowded, busy, noisy*, etc. Get learners to talk in pairs and ask one or two to share their answers with the class. You could also ask learners to write some True/False comparative sentences about their city and Tokyo for their partner to read and mark as true or false.

READING 1

PREPARING TO READ

PREVIEWING

1 👥 Set a time limit of 10–15 seconds for learners to preview the text quickly and answer the questions. Check answers with the class.

Answers

1 a questionnaire / a survey
2 to get information from people

USING YOUR KNOWLEDGE

2 👥 Remind learners that they can use what they already know about a topic to help them understand a text on that topic. Put learners in pairs and get them to ask and answer the questions (1–5). Check answers with the class.

Possible answers

1 in Thailand 2 a big city 3 Answers will vary.
4 Answers will vary. 5 very busy

Background note

Thailand, officially known as the Kingdom of Thailand, is in southeast Asia. The official language is Thai and the population is approximately 70 million. Bangkok is the capital of Thailand and is the largest city in the country with a population of over 8 million.

WHILE READING

Background note

The Reading 1 text is a questionnaire compiled by a group of students. In Unit 6, we saw an example of a questionnaire using a Likert scale. This questionnaire has a series of multiple-choice answers. Respondents answer the questions by ticking the correct boxes.

SKIMMING

3 👤 Focus on the questionnaire text. Remind learners that we skim to find the main topics and ideas of a text, not reading every word, but picking out important words. Ask learners to read the topics (1–6); you could check understanding of these by asking them to turn the phrases into direct questions, e.g. *How many hours do the people in Bangkok work or study? How do people travel in Bangkok?* Ask learners to skim the text and circle the topics covered by the survey. Check answers with the class.

> **Answers**
>
> Topics 2, 4, 5 and 6

SCANNING TO FIND INFORMATION

4 👤👥 Focus on the table and check understanding of the headings. Demonstrate the activity by eliciting one form of land transport. Set a time limit (up to four minutes) for the exercise to ensure learners scan the survey text. Learners complete the table by putting the forms of transport in the correct columns. Learners check their answers in pairs. Check answers with the class. Elicit another way of saying *go on foot* (= walk).

> **Answers**
>
> land transport: on foot, bicycle, car, tuk-tuk, motorbike, taxi, bus, SkyTrain, underground, train
> water transport: water taxi, boat, ferry
> air transport: plane

> **Background note**
>
> A *tuk-tuk* is a motorized three-wheeled rickshaw.

READING BETWEEN THE LINES

WORKING OUT MEANING FROM CONTEXT

Focus on the *Working out meaning from context* box. Explain that context means the topic of a text, its type and the words that are used in it. Thinking about the type of text (e.g. a questionnaire or survey) and the topic (e.g. transport) can help us understand the language in the text. When we see an unknown word, we can use the context as well as the words before and after the word to help us understand it.

5 👤 Focus on the highlighted words in the text and the definitions (1–6). Learners match the definitions to the highlighted words. Ask them to read the words around each highlighted word and think carefully about the whole context (i.e. a survey about transport use) and the immediate context (e.g. the questions for the person completing the survey). Demonstrate by matching the first word and definition with the whole class; draw attention to the words around *occupation* in the questionnaire (e.g. *What do you do? study, work*). Learners match the other words to the correct definitions. Check answers with the class. Model and drill pronunciation of any difficult words, e.g. *survey* /ˈsɜːveɪ/ and *gender* /ˈdʒendə/. Point out that *means* (= form, type, method) is singular.

> **Answers**
>
> 1 occupation 2 underground 3 survey
> 4 complete 5 means 6 gender

DISCUSSION

6 👥 Learners ask and answer the questions in pairs. You could also ask more able learners/fast finishers to talk about any problems with transport in their city/town for question 1. For feedback, ask one or two pairs to share their answers with the class. Elicit reasons for choosing certain types of transport for each category in question 2 from the whole class and revise comparative and superlative forms.

READING 2

PREPARING TO READ

PREVIEWING

1 👤 Allow 10–15 seconds for learners to preview the text and the visuals and answer the questions. Check answers with the class and ask further questions to check understanding, e.g. *Which city is the report about?* (Bangkok) *Where does the student study?* (At Bangkok University of Science and Technology.)

> **Answers**
>
> 1 b 2 c 3 a

UNDERSTANDING KEY VOCABULARY

2 👤 Ask learners to read the sentences (1–7) and complete them with the words from the box, using the glossary on page 200 to help them. Check answers with the class. Model and drill pronunciation of any difficult words, e.g. *percentage* /pəˈsentɪdʒ/ and *results* /rɪˈzʌlts/. You could teach *per cent* as well as *percentage* here as this comes up in Reading 2, e.g. *14% of people ride motorbikes.*

> **Answers**
>
> 1 percentage 2 pie chart 3 prefer   4 full of
> 5 spend 6 traffic jam   7 results

> **Language note**
>
> Note that *spend* collocates with time words as well as with money words, e.g. *spend time/an evening/an hour.*
>
> We use *to* with *prefer* to describe a preference between two things, e.g. *I prefer X to Y.*
>
> A *pie chart* /ˈpaɪ tʃɑːt/ is so named because it resembles a round pie divided into portions.

WHILE READING

SCANNING TO FIND INFORMATION

3 👤 Focus on the pie chart (Figure 1) and ask questions to check learners' understanding, e.g. *What percentage of people in Bangkok take/use the river taxi? (11%) What percentage walk to work / go to work on foot? (3%).* Focus on the missing percentages in the pie chart and elicit one missing percentage as an example. Ask learners to scan the text and complete the remaining gaps. Check answers with the class.

> **Answers**
>
> bicycle 2% car 22% tuk-tuk 8%
> motorbike 14% bus 18% SkyTrain 21%

READING FOR DETAIL

4 👤 Focus on the questions (1–5) and ask learners to read the text again closely in order to answer them. Check answers with the class. Ask what learners think the SkyTrain is (a train that travels on rails high above the streets).

If possible, show learners a picture of it from the Internet. Ask: *How long do you spend travelling to school/university/work?*

> **Answers**
>
> 1 over 12 million
> 2 a public form of transport
> 3 Yes, most people use them to get to work.
> 4 more than 1 hour
> 5 35%

> **Background note**
>
> The SkyTrain, officially known as the Bangkok Mass Transit System, is an elevated railway system. It has 32 stations and two lines that run for a total of 55 kilometres (32.5 miles).

UNDERSTANDING DISCOURSE

Remind learners that *discourse* means the way in which longer texts are built up and the way that the meanings of sentences are linked. Explain that when we write a text, instead of repeating the same word many times, we can substitute another word such as a pronoun or a more general word that refers to the same thing. Exercise 5 gives learners practice in this.

5 👤 Focus on the gapped text about Bangkok. Learners complete the text with the words/phrases in the box. The words in bold will help them to decide which to choose. Read the first sentence aloud, or write it on the board. Elicit that the gap could be filled with *Bangkok* or, to avoid repeating it, another word with a similar meaning (= *the city*). Learners complete the rest of the text. Slower learners may need more support here so monitor closely. Check answers with the class. If it is appropriate for your class, you can talk about the different words used in the text to refer to other words: *it* is used to refer to *the pie chart*; *who* is a relative pronoun which refers to *people*; *vehicle* is a general term for all kinds of wheeled road transport, including cars, buses, lorries and motorbikes.

> **Answers**
>
> 1 the city 2 It 3 who 4 Another way
> 5 the city 6 vehicle

⊙ LANGUAGE DEVELOPMENT

Quantifiers

Focus on the *Quantifiers* explanation box. These quantifiers are used with plural countable nouns to express quantities. The examples in the box are given in order, from lowest (*a few*) to highest (*most*). You could show this on the board by drawing a line with *a few* at one end and *most* at the other. Ask individual learners to write the other quantifiers on the correct places on the line.

Language note

These quantifiers are determiners, i.e. they determine how many/how much of a noun there is. The following quantifiers can be used with countable or uncountable nouns: *some*, *a lot of* and *most*. They answer the question *How much/many?* The following quantifiers can only be used with plural countable nouns: *a few*, *not many* and *many*. They answer the question *How many?*

Optional activity

Draw a pie chart divided into sections of different sizes on the board and write numbered sentences using *some*, *not many*, etc. in a list beside it. Ask learners to match each sentence to the correct slice of pie chart. Draw another pie chart with different-sized sections and label these with different kinds of drink, e.g. *tea, coffee, cola, water, juice, milk*. Then ask learners to write sentences using the quantifiers to describe it, e.g. *A few people like water. Not many people like milk*, etc.

1 ⋆ Ask learners to read the sentences (1–5), circling the quantifier in each sentence and underlining the noun which it refers to. Demonstrate the exercise by doing the first one together with the class. Check answers with the class.

Answers

1 quantifier: *Most*; noun: *people*
2 quantifier: *Some*; noun: *people*
3 quantifier: *Not many*; noun: *people*
4 quantifier: *A few*; noun: *people*
5 quantifier: *Many*; noun: *people*

2 ⋆⋆⋆ Focus on the sentences (1–5). Elicit suggestions for possible quantifiers to complete the first sentence. Remind learners that more than one answer is possible. Learners complete the other sentences, then compare their answers with a partner. Check answers with the class, eliciting any possible alternatives.

Answers

1 Many / Most / A lot of
2 Not many / A few
3 some (not many / a few)
4 Some (Not many / A few)
5 Not many / A few

TRANSPORT COLLOCATIONS

Remind learners that collocations are words that we often use together. (You could see if learners can remember any of the collocations for meals or daily routines, introduced in Unit 3.) Focus on the tables and highlight the key collocations here:

> *take* with forms of transport
> *to + school/work* (revise the use of the zero article in these expressions; but remind learners to use the article *the* with other places, e.g. *shops, city, shopping mall*)
> *by* + forms of transport, but remind learners of *on foot*; point out that these collocations with *by* do not have an article (*a/an/the*) before the noun (by the bus) *get* and *to* collocate here (= to reach) (but not get from)

Demonstrate making a sentence from the first table and elicit further sentences from learners.

Optional activity

⋆⋆ Put learners in pairs and ask them to make correct sentences from the table. Elicit more similar collocations and write them on the board, e.g. *by plane, by ferry, by train; to the shops, to the airport*, etc. Ask one or two pairs to share their new sentences with the class.

3 ⋆ Focus on the jumbled sentences (1–6). Ask learners to put the words in the correct order to make sentences, using the tables to help them. Check answers with the class.

Answers

1 We take a bus to school.
2 Malai travels to work by train.
3 Sunan takes his car to the city.
4 Many people get to work by motorbike.
5 My children get to school by bicycle.
6 Suni takes a taxi to the mall.

4 ⋆ Ask learners to complete the sentences (1–5) with the correct verbs from the box. Check answers with the class. You could elicit why the

verbs in questions 3 and 5 do not have third person -s. (In question 3, the verb comes after the modal auxiliary *can*; in question 5, the verb is an infinitive after *to*.)

| Answers

1 rides
2 flies
3 ride
4 takes
5 drive

CRITICAL THINKING

Go through the instructions with the class and focus on the writing task. Explain that the following sections of the unit will help them to prepare to write a paragraph about transport in their city.

UNDERSTAND

Collecting data

Focus on the *Collecting data* explanation box and explain that before writing a factual text, we usually need to collect information or data for it. Before they write their paragraph about transport in their city, learners will need to find out how people travel in their local area, using a questionnaire or survey.

1 ♟ Focus on the wordbox. Learners can check the meaning of new words in their dictionaries. Ask learners to choose six forms of transport that are popular in their city. (They can also choose a type of transport which is only found in their city and has a particular name, e.g. SkyTrain.) Focus on the gapped questionnaire and elicit the correct places for types of transport in the questionnaire (i.e. question 2 and Table 1). Learners complete the questionnaire with their transport words.

| Answers

Students' own answers

APPLY

2 ♟ Learners make copies of the questionnaire on page 187, enough for every other learner in the class (or it may be easier for you to do this for them). Learners distribute their surveys, complete the surveys of their classmates, and return them.

3 ♟ Ask learners to read the results and add up the numbers of people for each option. Ask them to use these numbers to work out the percentages and then make two pie charts showing the results of Questions 1 and 2. (Learners can either use computers to create these or draw them by hand if they prefer.) For example, if 7 out of 12 students take 5–15 minutes to get to school, they can work out the percentage by dividing 7 by 12 and multiplying it by 100 ($7 \div 12 = 0.58 \times 100 = 58\%$). Demonstrate using an example pie chart on the board, if necessary.

4 ♟ Ask learners to look at their results for Question 3 of the survey. Learners complete the sentences (1–3) with true information, e.g.:

Most students in my class never use a taxi.

Some students in my class always go by train.

A few people in my class sometimes walk / travel on foot.

WRITING

GRAMMAR FOR WRITING

Subject – Verb – Object

You could lead into this by revising work done in Unit 3. Write two sentences on the board, one with an object and one with a prepositional phrase. Ask learners to identify the object and the prepositional phrase, e.g.:

Abdullah studies Engineering.
(object: *Engineering*)

Abdullah lives in Cairo.
(prepositional phrase: *in Cairo*)

Focus on the *Subject – Verb – Object* explanation box and revise the typical word order of an English sentence. Highlight the fact that the last two example sentences each contain two prepositional phrases and ask learners to identify them: *to school + by metro, to school + by car*. These prepositional phrases answer the questions *Where?* (*to* + place) and *How?* (*by* + method). Point out the word order here: place first (*to school*) then method (*by metro / by car*).

1 ♟ Focus on the sentences (1–5) and elicit the first answer as an example. Learners decide whether the remaining bold words are objects or not. Check answers with the class.

Answers

1 Sentence 2 (*ferry*) and Sentence 4 (*motorbike*) have objects.

2 👤 Focus on the sentences (1–5) and explain that only three have objects. Learners find and underline them. Check answers with the class and elicit the verbs that come before each of these objects (*drives, ride, take*).

Answers

2 Hamdan drives <u>a car</u> to university.
4 Many commuters ride <u>a bicycle</u> to work in London.
5 People in Bangkok prefer to take <u>the SkyTrain</u>.

3 👥 Put learners in pairs and ask them to correct the mistakes in the sentences. You could elicit the first answer as an example. Check answers with the class. Ask learners to find objects in any of these sentences (sentence 3 *the metro*, sentence 4 *a motorbike*). Focus on / Revise the key language points here, if necessary, e.g. word order of prepositional phrases, i.e. place followed by method (sentences 1 and 4), omission of article in transport collocations with *by* (sentence 2), subject – verb – object word order (sentence 4) and agreement of noun and verb (sentence 5)

Answers

1 In Abu Dhabi, commuters travel <u>to work by car</u>.
2 Not many people in Ankara travel to work by <u>a</u> taxi.
3 Commuters in Seoul take the metro <u>to</u> work.
4 Most students <u>ride a motorbike to school</u>.
5 Some students in Paris <u>drive</u> to university.

Linking sentences with pronouns

Lead into this by revising the referencing covered in previous units, i.e. pronouns linking back to subjects in preceding sentences. Elicit examples of pronouns. Ask: *What do we use pronouns for?* Focus on the *Linking sentences with pronouns* explanation box. Show how pronouns can refer back to the subject or the object of a preceding sentence by putting the examples on the board and showing the links with arrows.

4 👤👥 Focus on the sentences (1–5) and (a–e) and draw attention to the bold words. Elicit the first matching pair of sentences from the class. Point out how *They* refers back to *Jamila and Kamilah*. Learners match the remaining sentences, then check their answers in pairs. Check answers with the class. You could put/ project the exercise onto the board and

show how the pronouns link back to the preceding nouns by drawing arrows, e.g. 2 *He* to *Hamdan*, 3 *They* to *Some people*, 4 *It* to *a bicycle*, 5 *It* to *SkyTrain*.

Answers

1 d 2 a 3 e 4 c 5 b

5 👤 Focus on the pairs of sentences (1–5) and draw attention to the bold words. Elicit the first pronoun as an example and show the way *It* refers back to *plane*. Learners complete the remaining sentences with suitable pronouns. Remind them to look at the bold words to help them. Check answers with the class.

Answers

1 It 2 It 3 They 4 They 5 It

ACADEMIC WRITING SKILLS

Error correction

Focus on the *Error correction* explanation box. Explain the codes by going through the examples with the class. Write up an incorrect sentence and ask a confident learner to come and mark it using the codes, then ask another learner to correct it, e.g.

> Not many people Paris <u>travels</u> to work by taxi.
>
> [MW] *in* [G] *travel*

Discuss the errors and the corrections with learners.

👤 Focus on the pie chart and the student's paragraph. Elicit the correction to the first mistake and discuss it with the class. Learners correct the remaining mistakes. Remind them to look at the pie chart for the correct information to correct errors of content (C). Check answers with the class. If learners had problems with any particular language points, revise these with the class.

Answers

The pie chart (Figure 1) <u>shows</u> [G] popular means of transport for students <u>in</u> [MW] Madrid. There are five types of transport: bicycle, bus, car, taxi <u>and</u> [MW] train. <u>Most</u> [P] <u>people</u> [G] travel <u>by</u> [WP] bus (<u>45%</u>) [C]. Bicycles <u>are</u> [MW] also very popular. 33% of students travel to school by <u>a</u> [G] bicycle. Students prefer cars but more students own bicycles than cars. 7% of <u>students</u> [G] drive <u>to</u> [WP] school. Students do not take <u>the train / taxis</u> [MW] to school. Buses are the <u>most</u> [G] popular form of transport for students in Madrid.

WRITING TASK

PLAN

1 Ask learners to read the results of their surveys and their pie charts from the Critical thinking section.

2 Tell learners that they are going to use their survey results to write about transport in their city. Point out that the three gapped phrases here are: 1 the title for their paragraph, and 2 and 3 the titles (or captions) for the two pie charts, Figure 1 and 2, that they will include as part of their report. Learners complete the gapped titles/captions with the name of their city.

3 Focus on the gapped introduction and ask learners to complete it with the name of their city and its population (learners may need to research the population using the Internet first).

4 Focus on the prompts (1–5). Elicit examples of the first sentence, e.g. *The six forms of transport in the survey are ... .* As learners are writing only three or four sentences about six means of transport, point out that they will need to combine some statements using *and* or *but*, e.g. *60% of students take buses but only 5% go to school on foot.* Elicit examples of comparative sentences for question 3 using *more popular than.* The model paragraph on page 190 has *More students own bicycles than cars* and *Buses are the more popular form of transport* which you could highlight as models for stronger learners.
Learners write further sentences following the prompts. Monitor and help as required.

WRITE A FIRST DRAFT

5 Ask learners to combine their introduction (from Exercise 3) with the sentences they wrote for Exercise 4 and the pie charts they created from their survey results to make a paragraph. Remind them where possible to link sentences with pronouns to avoid repeating subjects and objects and to make their paragraph flow well (see the *Grammar for writing* section).

EDIT

6 Focus on the task checklist. Go through the checklist to make sure learners know what to check. Then ask learners to edit their work, using the checklist to help them.

7 Learners swap paragraphs with a partner who reads it and marks any corrections using the error correction codes from page 190. Learners discuss their corrections with their partners. Learners then use their partner's corrections to write a final draft of their paragraph for handing in to you. These paragraphs could be displayed around the classroom for other learners to look at.

Answers
See page 140 for a model answer.

OBJECTIVES REVIEW
See Introduction, page 9, for ideas about using the Objectives Review with your learners.

WORDLIST
See Introduction, page 9, for ideas about how to make the most of the Wordlist with your learners.

REVIEW TEST
See page 127 for the photocopiable Review Test for this unit and page 94, for ideas about when and how to administer the Review Test.

RESEARCH PROJECT

Plan an exhibition called, 'Transport, past and present'.

As a class, explain that the learners will be setting up an exhibition. They should brainstorm the different parts of the exhibition and allocate these to different teams. They should also consider who the visitors will be, the location, marketing and the date.

Learners should also think about activities in the exhibition, sourcing images, producing videos and perhaps inviting relatives or specialists to talk about means of transport in the past.

The review tests are designed to be used after the learners have completed each unit of the Student's book. Each Review test checks learners' knowledge of the key language areas taught in the unit and practices the reading skills from the unit. The Review tests take 50 minutes to complete but you may wish to adjust this time depending on your class or how much of the Student's book unit you covered. Review tests can be given as homework as general revision. Photocopy one test for each learner. Learners should do the tests on their own. You can check the answers by giving learners each other's papers to mark or correct the papers yourself. Keep a record of the results to help monitor individual learner progress.

REVIEW TEST 1 ANSWERS

Reading
1 1 Usain 2 Bolt 3 Jamaica 4 Kingston 5 1986
2 1 is / comes 2 lives 3 brother 4 is 5 runs

Vocabulary
3 1 clothes 2 family 3 languages 4 height 5 football
4 1 son 2 grandfather 3 uncle 4 daughter 5 aunt

Language development: Nouns and verbs
5 1 **is:** *verb*
   2 **policeman:** *noun*
   3 **lives:** *verb*
   4 **works:** *verb*
   5 **hobbies:** *noun*

Language development: Singular and plural nouns
6 1 brothers 2 shoes 3 hobby 4 aunts 5 sister

Grammar for writing: The verb be
7 1 is 2 am 3 am 4 is 5 is 6 is 7 is 8 are 9 is 10 is

Grammar for writing: Possessive determiners
8 1 Their 2 Her 3 Our 4 My 5 His

Academic writing skills
9 1 My uncle is Ahmed. 2 He is 49. 3 He is a dentist.
   4 He is from Jeddah. 5 He has two sons.

REVIEW TEST 2 ANSWERS

Reading
1 1 i January to March 2 c June to August 3 b 16 4 h
   June 5 d nine 6 f 15 7 g during the dry winter 8 a
   153 mm 9 j 14 10 e 1952

Vocabulary
2 1 rainfall 2 speed 3 warm 4 temperature 5 sunny

Language development: Adjectives and nouns
3 adjectives: difficult, warm, closed, cold, young
   nouns: Maths, classroom, university, weather, brothers

Language development: Noun phrases
4 1 tropical climate 2 warm classroom 3 good film
   4 high rainfall 5 young sister
5 1 I have a young brother.
   2 In winter, the weather is cold.
   3 Spain has a good climate.
   4 The rainy season is from November to February.
   5 The average temperature is 15 °C in spring.

Academic writing skills: Subject and verb
6 1 d 2 e 3 a 4 c 5 b

Academic writing skills: Prepositions
7 1 in 2 from 3 in 4 in 5 to
8 1 The weather is good in the dry season.
   2 In August, it is warm.
   3 The winters are cold in Moscow.
   4 In South Africa, the climate is good.
   5 Kemal lives in Ankara in Turkey.

REVIEW TEST 3 ANSWERS

Reading
1 1 this week 2 journalist 3 full-time 4 London
   5 9 am 6 website 7 four 8 friendly 9 no
   experience 10 loves

Vocabulary
2 1 early 2 amazing 3 morning 4 lifestyle 5 late
   6 hunt 7 village 8 cook 9 different 10 traditional

Language development: Collocations
3 1 early 2 coffee 3 the train 4 Physics 5 the cinema
4 1 e Maria has a shower every morning.
   2 i My father reads a book on the train to work.
   3 b Maria and Stefanos get up late and have
      breakfast together at 10 am!
   4 g Fred eats his lunch in the café.
   5 a Danae goes to the gym twice a week.
   6 j My grandmother cooks dinner on a Sunday.
   7 c Chloe and Annabel relax with friends in the
      evenings.
   8 f Mayur does his homework in the evening.
   9 h Susan lives with her sister.
   10 d Toshihiro goes to bed at 1 am.

Grammar for writing: Subject – Verb – Object

5

subject	object
I	my teeth
Bill	his homework
My tutor	questions
Olivia	Economics
Sarah	orange juice

Grammar for writing: Time expressions

6 1 on 2 at 3 on 4 In 5 at

Academic writing skills: Spelling

7 1 Maths 2 English 3 Physics 4 Engineering 5 Biology

REVIEW TEST 4 ANSWERS

Reading

1 continents: Europe, Africa, America
nationalities: Turkish, Indian

2 1 False 2 True 3 True 4 False 5 False 6 False
7 True 8 False 9 True 10 False

Vocabulary: Places in a country

3 1 Desert 2 beach 3 field 4 mountains 5 Lake
6 rivers 7 Sea 8 forest 9 Ocean 10 modern

Grammar for writing: *There is / There are*

4 1 There is a big factory in my city.
2 There are over 700 different kinds of British cheese.
3 There are many museums in Paris.
4 There is a large mosque in Lahore.
5 There are over 850 languages in Papua New Guinea.

Grammar for writing: articles

5 1 The Lake Como is in Italy.
2 He comes from the Morocco.
3 Lots of people live in the New York.
4 There are many modern buildings in the United Arab Emirates.
5 Cambodia is in the Asia.

Academic writing skills: Spelling and punctuation

6 1 Chinese 2 Egyptian 3 French 4 Indian
5 Japanese 6 Saudi
7 Thai 8 Emirati 9 British 10 Turkish

7 1 There are three main islands in New Zealand.
2 The climate is good in Malta.
3 Seafood is very popular in Greece.
4 He comes from Northern Ireland.
5 There are a lot of interesting museums in Berlin.

REVIEW TEST 5 ANSWERS

Reading

1 1 False 2 True 3 True 4 False 5 False 6 True
7 False 8 True
9 True 10 False

Vocabulary

2 1 million 2 player 3 local 4 everywhere 5 boring
6 national
7 dangerous 8 ticket 9 safe 10 fan

Language development: Sports collocations

3 1 go horse-riding
2 go swimming
3 play baseball
4 do exercise
5 play cricket
6 play rugby
7 play squash
8 go jogging
9 play basketball
10 do karate

Language development: Prepositions

4 1 in 2 on 3 in 4 on 5 in

Language development: Adjectives

5 cheap – expensive
easy – difficult
dangerous – safe
hard – soft
boring – exciting

Grammar for writing: Subject – Verb – Adjective

6 1 Karate is dangerous.
2 Basketball is popular in Russia.
3 Ki Sung-Yueng is a famous football player in Korea.
4 Cricket is not popular in Albania.
5 Tickets for the final are expensive.

Grammar for writing: Subject – Verb – Adverb

7 1 People go horse-riding in the park.
2 Swimming lessons are on Thursday evenings.
3 We play cricket on the beach.
4 In summer, we play tennis.
5 I go jogging on Tuesdays.

REVIEW TEST 6 ANSWERS

Reading

1 1 False 2 True 3 False 4 True 5 False

2 1 Z 2 A 3 Z 4 P 5 W

Vocabulary: Jobs

3 1 healthy 2 fit 3 fluent 4 part-time 5 friendly 6 full-time 7 link 8 soon 9 fitness instructor 10 long hours

Language development: Vocabulary for jobs

4 1 An accountant looks after money in a company.
   2 A window cleaner cleans windows on buildings.
   3 A builder builds houses in towns and cities.
   4 A chef prepares food in a restaurant.
   5 A doctor gives people medicine in hospital.
   6 A pilot flies planes to different countries.
   7 A fireman puts out fires in towns and cities.
   8 A flight attendant looks after passengers on a plane.
   9 An astronaut flies spacecraft in space.
   10 A vet looks after animals in farms and zoos.

Language development: Adjective phrases

5 1 kind and patient 2 beautiful 3 smart 4 creative 5 good with computers 6 good with people 7 creative 8 intelligent 9 fit and strong 10 good with people

Grammar for writing: *must* and *have to*

6 1 A dentist does not / doesn't have to be strong.
   2 A chef has to be good with food.
   3 Nurses have to be good with people.
   4 Actors have to be creative.
   5 A builder does not have to be good with computers.

Academic writing skills: Contractions

7 1 I am very tired. 2 I hope you are better. 3 Simone is a good friend. 4 Julia is a clever student. 5 Jack does not have to work on Monday.

REVIEW TEST 7 ANSWERS

Reading

1 1 True 2 True 3 False 4 True 5 True 6 False 7 False 8 False 9 True 10 True

Language development: Vocabulary for buildings

2 1 Hotel 2 cinema 3 hospital 4 ice rink 5 shopping mall 6 Stadium 7 Library 8 train station 9 Museum 10 swimming pool

Vocabulary for parts of buildings

3 When you arrive at the hotel, you can leave your car in the underground car park. Enter the building through the entrance and ride on the escalator to the top floor. On the top floor, you go up the stairs to café in the roof garden. If there's a fire or another emergency, leave the building by the nearest exit.

Adjectives

4 ugly – beautiful
   cheap – expensive
   narrow – wide
   small – big
   new – old

Grammar for writing: Comparing quantities and comparative adjectives

5 1 The Metropolitan Museum of Art is more popular than the Museum of Modern Art.
   2 The Chadstone Shopping Centre in Melbourne is more of modern than the Westfield Bondi Junction in Sydney.
   3 The Shard is smaller than the Burj Khalifa.
   4 Skyscrapers are uglier than old buildings.
   5 Taipei 101 is taller than the Empire State Building.
   6 Gold is more expensive than paper.
   7 This street is many narrower than the main road.
   8 Tokyo is busier than Vancouver.
   9 The island of Sri Lanka is bigger than the island of Sicily.
   10 The old market is more beautiful than the new shopping mall.

6 1 The Savoy Hotel has more restaurants and bars than the Hotel de Crillon but the Hotel de Crillon is older.
   2 Shinjuku train station is busier than Grand Central Terminal but Grand Central Terminal has more platforms.
   3 The Al Wahda shopping mall is bigger than the Westfield shopping mall but the Westfield shopping mall is newer.
   4 The Crystal Lagoon is longer than the Marina Sands Skypark swimming pool but the Marina Sands Skypark swimming pool is higher.
   5 The BFI IMAX cinema has a bigger screen than Cinesphere but Cinesphere can seat more people.

Academic writing skills: Spelling: double consonants

7 1 shopping 2 cinema 3 swimming 4 restaurant 5 running

REVIEW TEST 8 ANSWERS

Reading

1 1 False 2 True 3 False 4 False 5 True

2 1 Over 70
   2 Ethiopia or southern Arabia
   3 Coffee spread through the Arab world to Turkey, Italy, and then through Europe to Britain.
   4 Coffee with milk or cream
   5 In the morning for breakfast, during a coffee break in the middle of the morning, after a meal

Language development: Vocabulary for food and drink

3 1 potatoes 2 milk 3 honey 4 coconut 5 yoghurt 6 onion 7 spices 8 water 9 almonds 10 dates

Language development: Countable and uncountable nouns

4 countable nouns: potatoes, dates, onion, chillies, spices

uncountable nouns: milk, honey, butter, yoghurt, water

Grammar for writing: Subject–Verb agreement

5
1. Arab restaurants <u>serve</u> *sharwarma* and *kabsa*.
2. Cambodian cuisine <u>uses</u> a lot of fruit.
3. Seafood <u>is</u> popular in many restaurants in Greece.
4. A famous dish from Korea <u>is</u> *kim chee*.
5. Two popular dishes in Turkey <u>are</u> called *dolma* and *gözleme*.
6. Thai food <u>is</u> served with rice and vegetables.
7. Moroccan chefs <u>prepare</u> *tajine* dishes.
8. Kebabs <u>are</u> served in pita bread.
9. Indian chefs <u>make</u> curries with vegetables and spices.
10. Rice <u>is</u> popular in Japan.

Grammar for writing: Determiners: *a*, *an* and *some*

6
1. <u>A</u> popular rice dish in Spain is *paella*.
2. There are some <u>potatoes</u> in *Lancashire hotpot*.
3. <u>Italians</u> like eating pizza and pasta.
4. Ethiopian chefs <u>prepare</u> *tibs* with meat and some vegetables.
5. Turkish cooks add <u>an</u> egg to *menemen*.

Academic writing skills: Spelling

7 1 sweet 2 savoury 3 delicious 4 spicy 5 healthy

REVIEW TEST 9 ANSWERS

Reading

1
1. A safe place for animals to live
2. An Indian elephant is smaller than an African elephant and it has smaller ears.
3. In national parks
4. 2,000
5. They live in mountain forests in southwest India.

2

scientific name	Elephas maximus indicus	Panthera tigris	Macaca silenus
common name	Indian Elephant	Royal Bengal Tiger	Lion-tailed Macaque
size (cm)	Males: 2–3.5 m	Males: 275–290 cm	40–60 cm tails: 25 cm
weight (kg)	2,000–5,000 kg	135–230 kg	3–10 kg
lifespan (years)	50–70 years old	10–15 years old	30 years in zoos, shorter lifespan in the wild
food	plants (150 kg every day)	meat (up to 40 kg at one time)	leaves, fruit and nuts

Vocabulary

3 nouns: cubs, prey

verbs: run, catch, hunt

Language development: *can* and *cannot*

4
1. Lions can <u>survive</u> without water for four or five days.
2. Lions can ~~to~~ <u>communicate</u> with other lions by roaring.
3. You can <u>hear</u> a lion roar from 8 km away.
4. A male lion <u>can</u> weigh 250 kg.
5. Lions <u>cannot</u> run for long distances.

Language development: Describing facts about animals

5 1 in 2 at 3 for 4 at 5 on

Vocabulary for animals

6 1 venomous 2 amphibious 3 endangered 4 harmless 5 nocturnal

Grammar for writing: Superlative adjectives

7
1. The cheetah is the fastest animal in the world. / The fastest animal in the world is the cheetah.
2. The sea snake is the most venomous snake. / The most venomous snake is the sea snake.
3. The Ulysses butterfly is one of the most beautiful butterflies in the world.
4. Tiger sharks are one of the deadliest fish in the world.
5. The whale shark is the biggest fish in the world. / The biggest fish in the world is the whale shark.

Academic writing skills: Spelling

8 1 bear 2 bird 3 bat 4 wolf 5 insect 6 falcon 7 bee 8 spider 9 shark 10 lion

Academic writing skills: Punctuation

9
1. Many dangerous animals live in South America.
2. One of the most dangerous fish in South America is the piranha.
3. Piranhas live in South American rivers like the Amazon and the Orinoco.
4. They normally grow between 14 and 26 cm long.
5. Piranhas eat insects, fish and small animals.

REVIEW TEST 10 ANSWERS

Reading

1 1 True 2 False 3 False 4 True 5 False

Language development: Quantifiers

2 1 *Many / Most / A lot of* (83%) people in Florida drive to work.

2 *Not many / A few* (4%) people in Florida walk to work.

3 *Not many / A few* (2%) people in Florida take public transport to work.

4 *Not many / A few* (1.5%) people in Florida ride a bike to work.

5 *Not many / A few* (3%) people in California ride a bike to work.

6 *Many / Most / A lot of* (74%) people in California drive to work.

7 *Not many / A few* (5%) people in California take public transport to work.

8 *Some* (27%) people in New York take public transport to work.

9 *Not many / A few* (7%) people in New York walk to work.

10 *Not many / A few* (4%) people in Texas walk to work.

Language development: Transport collocations

3 1 to 2 by 3 from 4 to 5 by

4 1 rides 2 drives 3 rides 4 takes 5 ride

Grammar for writing: Subject – Verb – Object

5 1 Commuters in Paris take the metro <u>to</u> work.

2 Some commuters in Japan travel <u>by</u> plane.

3 Many commuters in Istanbul go <u>by</u> (or <u>take the</u>) ferry to work.

4 In Saigon, families often <u>ride</u> a motorbike (or <u>travel by motorbike</u>) to work and school.

5 Some students in California <u>drive</u> to university.

6 A few students <u>take</u> the bus.

7 Most students <u>ride a bike to college</u>.

8 Not many people in Dhaka travel to work by <u>a</u> taxi.

9 Many commuters in Sydney <u>take/get</u> the train to work.

10 In Dubai, commuters <u>travel to work by car</u>.

Grammar for writing: Linking sentences with pronouns

6 1 c 2 e 3 d 4 a 5 b

Academic writing skills: Error correction

7 The table <u>shows</u> [G] how <u>Americans</u> [P] commute to work. There are five types of transport: driving a car alone, sharing a car, taking public transport, cycling and walking. In 43 states, more <u>than</u> [MW] 75% of <u>commuters</u> [C] drive a car alone <u>to</u> [MW] work. In <u>New York</u> [P], 50% of <u>commuters</u> [G] use other ways to get <u>to</u> [WP] work. About 14% of commuters share a car to work in Alaska and Hawaii, the highest percentage in the <u>USA.</u> [C] Most people in New York use public transport. Here, 28% take a train, subway or bus. In Alabama, Arkansas, Maine and Mississippi, 1% of commuters use public transport. Bicycling and walking are not popular forms of public transport <u>in</u> [WP] the USA.

REVIEW TEST 1

Name: .... **Date:** ....

READING (10 marks)

> *Unusual people*: Chapter 8 – Fastest and slowest
>
> **A VERY fast man!**
>
> Usain Bolt is from Jamaica. He was born in 1986. He lives in Kingston, Jamaica. He lives with his brother.
>
> Usain is an athlete. He runs very fast. He runs in 100-metre and 200-metre races. He was good at running at school. He is the fastest runner in the world. He is called the fastest man of all time.
>
> Usain is a world-record holder for the 100 metres and 200 metres. He has six Olympic gold medals. Three are from the 2008 Beijing Olympics and three are from the 2012 London Olympics.
>
> Usain works very hard. He runs and he goes to the gym. He runs in races all over the world. He went to Daegu in Korea in 2011. He went to London in the UK in 2012.

1 Circle the correct options.

> **Profile: Usain Bolt**
> First name: (1)*Usain / Bolt*
> Last name: (2)*Usain / Bolt*
> Country: (3)*Korea / Jamaica*
> City: (4)*London / Kingston*
> Date of birth: (5)*1968 / 1986*

2 Read the text again. Write the correct words from the text in the gaps.

1 Usain Bolt _____ from Jamaica.

2 He _____ in Kingston.

3 He lives with his _____ .

4 Usain _____ an athlete.

5 He _____ very fast.

VOCABULARY (10 marks)

3 Write the words from the box in the gaps. You do not need every word.

> football hobby family farmer clothes shoes height languages

1 When it is cold, we wear warm _____ .

2 John has three brothers and three sisters. He has a large _____ .

3 Carlos speaks two _____ : Spanish and English.

4 He is not tall or short. He is average _____ .

5 My favourite _____ club is Manchester United.

4 Write the words from the box in the gaps. You do not need every word.

| grandfather   grandmother   uncle   aunt   brother   sister   mother   father   daughter   son |

1 My brother is my mother's _____ .
2 My father's father is my _____ .
3 My mother's brother is my _____ .
4 My sister is my father's _____ .
5 My mother's sister is my _____ .

LANGUAGE DEVELOPMENT (10 marks)

NOUNS AND VERBS

5 Circle the correct option (noun or verb) for each bold word.

1 Istanbul **is** a big city. *noun / verb*
2 Peter is a **policeman**. *noun / verb*
3 Jane **lives** in Dubai. *noun / verb*
4 Elena's mother **works** in Rome. *noun / verb*
5 Alberto's **hobbies** are dangerous. *noun / verb*

SINGULAR AND PLURAL NOUNS

6 Circle the correct words.

1 My father has four *brother / brothers*.
2 These *shoe / shoes* are too big.
3 My father has a *hobby / hobbies*.
4 I have two *aunt / aunts*.
5 They have a *sister / sisters*.

GRAMMER AND WRITING (15 marks)

THE VERB *BE*

7 Write *am, is* or *are* in the gaps.

My name (1) _____ Tomiko. I
(2) _____ from Osaka. I
(3) _____ 21. Osaka (4) _____
in Japan. My brother's name (5) _____
Hiroshi. He (6) _____ older. He
(7) _____ 26. His hobbies
(8) _____ swimming and playing
football. My father's name (9) _____
Azuma. He (10) _____ a bank manager.

POSSESSIVE DETERMINERS

8 Circle the correct words.

   1 I have two brothers. *Their / They* names are Yousef and Said.

   2 Nura is from Tunisia. *She / Her* father's name is Mohammad.

   3 We go to university in Berlin. *Our / Its* university is very big.

   4 I have a brother and a sister. *Her / My* sister's name is Charlotte.

   5 Hassan is from Birmingham. *Her / His* mother is from Pakistan.

ACADEMIC WRITING SKILLS (5 marks)

9 Put the words in order to make sentences.

   1 Ahmed / My uncle / is / .

_____

   2 is / He / 49 / .

_____

   3 a dentist / He / is / .

_____

   4 is from / He / Jeddah / .

_____

   5 two sons / He / has / .

_____

TOTAL _____/ 50

Name: .... **Date:** ....

READING (10 marks)

> **The Wettest Town in the World: Cilaos, Réunion**
>
> Cilaos is the wettest town in the world. It is on the French island of Réunion in the Indian Ocean. Cilaos is in the centre of the island in the mountains. In 1952, Cilaos had the wettest 24 hours ever recorded in the world. Between 15th and 16th March, there were 1,869.9 mm of rainfall.
>
> **Average temperatures in Cilaos**
>
> The temperatures in Cilaos are from 16 °C to 30 °C. The warmest months are January to March. The temperatures are from 22 °C to 30 °C. There are about 16 rainy days in January. The average rainfall in January is 153 mm.
>
> The coldest months are June to August. The temperatures are from 16 °C to 25 °C. On average there are only nine rainy days in May. The average rainfall in May is 39 mm.
>
> **Seasons in Cilaos**
>
> 'June is the start of the winter,' says George, 'and this is my favourite time of year.' George is a farmer. He grows fruit and sugarcane. He has two children. His daughter Angélique is 15. His son Serge is 14.
>
> **George has a dry house in a wet city**
>
> 'November is the beginning of the wet season. We can have big storms. These are called cyclones. The wettest months are January and February. The rain is heavy and regular. During the dry winter, I check the house. I fix the roof and get ready for the wet season,' George says.
>
> People in Cilaos like being outside in the dry season. In their free time, they go to the beach. When it is too hot, they go to the mountains to cool down.

1 Match the facts (1–10) to the correct words or numbers (a–j).

1	the warmest months	a	153 mm
2	the coldest months	b	16
3	the average number of rainy days in January	c	June to August
		d	nine
4	the start of winter	e	1952
5	the average number of rainy days in May	f	15
6	Angélique's age	g	during the dry winter
7	George checks the house	h	June
8	the average rainfall in January	i	January to March
9	Serge's age	j	14
10	the wettest 24 hours in the world		

VOCABULARY (5 marks)

2 Write the words from the box in the gaps. You do not need every word.

| speed   rainfall   climate   temperature   cold   windy   sunny   rainy   cloudy   warm |

1 South Africa is a dry country. It has an average _____ of about 464 mm a year.
2 The new Ferrari LaFerrari has a top _____ of more than 300 kph.
3 Egypt has _____ winters with an average temperature of 15 °C.
4 The highest _____ recorded in Australia is 50.7 °C.
5 I like sunbathing on a _____ day.

LANGUAGE DEVELOPMENT (20 marks)

ADJECTIVES AND NOUNS

3 Write the bold words in the correct places in the table.
   1 **Maths** is **difficult**.
   2 The **classroom** is **warm**.
   3 The **university** is **closed** in the holidays.
   4 The **weather** is **cold** today.
   5 I've got two **young brothers**.

adjectives	nouns

NOUN PHRASES

4 Make a noun phrase from the **bold** words in each sentence (1–5) and write it in the gaps.
   1 The **climate** is **tropical** in Vietnam.
     Vietnam has a _____ _____.

   2 The **classroom** is **warm**.
     We have a _____ _____.

   3 The **film** is **good**.
     It is a _____ _____.

   4 The **rainfall** in Cilaos is **high**.
     Cilaos has _____ _____.

   5 My **sister** is **young**.
     I have a _____ _____.

5 Correct the mistakes.

1 I have a brother young.

_____

2 In winter, the cold weather is.

_____

3 Spain has a climate good.

_____

4 The season is rainy is from November to February.

_____

5 The temperature is average is 15 °C in spring.

_____

ACADEMIC WRITING SKILLS (15 marks)

SUBJECT AND VERB

6 Match the sentence halves.

1 Usain Bolt	a **is** 153 mm.
2 Jamaica and Cuba	b **are** from the Czech Republic.
3 The average rainfall in January	c **is** open.
4 The university	d **is** an athlete.
5 Martina and Pavel	e **are** in the Caribbean.

PREPOSITIONS

7 Write the prepositions in the gaps.

to (x1)   from (x1)   in (x3)

1 Kingston is _____ Jamaica.
2 The average temperatures in Réunion are _____ 22 °C to 30 °C.
3 It is very rainy _____ the wet season.
4 Summers are hot _____ Australia.
5 The average temperatures are from 17 °C _____ 30°C.

8 Put the words in order to make sentences.

1 weather / the / good / dry / is / season / The / in / .

_____

2 warm / August / , / is / it / In / .

_____

3 Moscow / The / are / cold / winters / in / .

_____

4 South Africa / climate / good / the / is / In / , / .

_____

5 Turkey / Ankara / in / Kemal / in / lives / .

_____

TOTAL _____/ 50

REVIEW TEST 3

Name: .... Date: ....

READING (10 marks)

> **William's blog**
>
> *My first week at my new job*
>
> I started work this week as a journalist. It's my first full-time job. The job is at *The Highbury Herald*. It's in north London. It's a community news website with a monthly print magazine.
>
> I get up early and I start work at 9 am. I start the day in the office. Then I travel around London. I usually speak to people all day. I write my stories in the office. At the moment, all of my stories are for the website.
>
> Four other people work here. Tina is the editor. Jo and Sam are journalists. George works in accounts. Everyone is very friendly.
>
> The salary isn't very good but I'm new to journalism. The job gives me experience. Perhaps I can get a better-paid job when I have more experience. I love my new job because I meet lots of interesting people.

1 Circle the correct options.

William …

1   started a new job *this week / last week.*

2   is a *student / journalist.*

3   works *full-time / part-time.*

4   works in *London / Liverpool.*

5   starts work at *8.30 am / 9 am.*

6   writes stories for a *magazine / website.*

7   works with *three / four* people.

8   thinks everyone is *sad / friendly.*

9   has *no experience / a lot of experience.*

10   *loves / hates* his job.

VOCABULARY (10 marks)

2 Write the words from the box in the gaps. You do not need every word.

> different   traditional   imagine   hunt   amazing   lifestyle   jungle
> cook   morning   afternoon   evening   early   late   village

1   My grandmother gets up at 6 am. She likes to get up _____ .

2   I love this movie! The story is _____ !

3   Most people have breakfast in the _____ .

4   Belinda has a healthy _____ . She goes swimming three times a week.

5   Please be ready to leave at 6 pm. I don't want to arrive _____ .

6   Kombai men _____ animals in the forest.

7   I live in a small _____ . The nearest town is ten kilometres away.

8   I want to _____ dinner tonight. What would you like?

9 Canada and Mexico are very _____ countries. Canada is cold but Mexico is hot.

10 *Tajine* is a _____ meal in North Africa.

LANGUAGE DEVELOPMENT (15 marks)

3 Write the words from the box in the gaps.

the cinema   Physics   the train   coffee   early

1 Jake gets up _____ .

2 He has _____ for breakfast.

3 He takes _____ every morning.

4 Jake studies _____ at Cambridge University.

5 He goes to _____ every Saturday.

4 Match the sentence halves.

1 Maria has   ☐   a the gym twice a week.

2 My father reads   ☐   b breakfast together at 10 am!

3 Maria and Stefanos get up late
   and have   ☐   c with friends in the evenings.

4 Fred eats   ☐   d to bed at 1 am.

5 Danae goes to   ☐   e a shower every morning.

6 My grandmother cooks   ☐   f his homework in the evening.

7 Chloe and Annabel relax   ☐   g his lunch in the café.

8 Mayur does   ☐   h with her sister.

9 Susan lives   ☐   i a book on the train to work.

10 Toshihiro goes   ☐   j dinner on a Sunday.

GRAMMAR FOR WRITING (10 marks)

SUBJECT – VERB – OBJECT

5 Write the subject and object from each sentence in the correct columns of the table.

1 Every morning, I brush my teeth.

2 Bill does his homework on the bus!

3 My tutor asks questions.

4 Olivia studies Economics.

5 Sarah has orange juice for breakfast.

subject	object

TIME EXPRESSIONS

6 Write *at*, *in* or *on* in the gaps.

1 Mark plays football _____ Saturdays.

2 Silvia has an English class _____ 2 pm.

3 Jeremy goes to university _____ Tuesdays and Thursdays.

4 _____ the evening, Ksenia studies in the library.

5 Steve has a History lesson _____ 11 am.

ACADEMIC WRITING SKILLS (5 marks)

7 Correct the spellings of these university subjects.

1 Mathes _____

2 Englesh _____

3 Phisics _____

4 Enginering _____

5 Bilogy _____

TOTAL _____/ 50

REVIEW TEST 4

Name: .... **Date:** ....

READING (15 marks)

> **Piri Reis and his world map**
>
> Piri Reis came from Turkey. He was born in about 1465 and died in 1553. Piri Reis travelled around the Mediterranean Sea and the Arabian Gulf. He was a famous sea captain. Today he is famous for his world map.
>
> Piri Reis's world map comes from his *Book of Navigation* (1521). Most of the book is in Turkish. It has information on navigation and maps of ports and cities in the Mediterranean Sea.
>
> The book also has a world map. This world map shows parts of Europe, North Africa and South America. Piri Reis used older Arab, Spanish, Portuguese, Chinese, Indian and Greek maps to help him draw his world map. The map also shows the Azores and the Canary Islands in the Atlantic Ocean.
>
> Peri Reis became famous when part of his world map was found in the Topkapi Palace in Istanbul in 1929. It is the oldest Turkish world map. It is also one of the oldest maps of America.

1 Read the text and find the names of continents and nationalities. Circle them in the table.

continents	nationalities
Asia	Turkish
Australia	Swedish
Europe	Norwegian
Africa	Indian
America	French

2 Read the text and write true (T) or false (F) next to the statements below.

1 Piri Reis was Tunisian. _____
2 Piri Reis was a sea captain. _____
3 There are maps in the *Book of Navigation*. _____
4 The world map shows North America. _____
5 Piri Reis sailed to South America. _____
6 The *Book of Navigation* is in Portuguese. _____
7 Piri Reis's map is the oldest world Turkish map. _____
8 Piri Reis used French maps to help him draw his world map. _____
9 Piri Reis died in 1553. _____
10 The Canary Islands are in the Mediterranean Sea. _____

VOCABULARY (10 marks)

3 Write the words from the box in the gaps. You do not need every word.

| rivers | Lake | forest | Sea | Ocean | mountains | hill | Desert | beach | field | modern | cliff |

1 The Sahara _____ is in North Africa.

2 In the summer, we play football on the _____ and swim in the sea.

3 The farmer's cows are in the _____ .

4 The biggest _____ are in the Himalayas.

5 _____ Titicaca is in South America.

6 The Thames and the Mississippi are famous _____ .

7 The Adriatic _____ is between Italy and the Balkans.

8 A large area with many trees is a _____ .

9 The South Atlantic _____ is between America and Africa.

10 Abu Dhabi is a _____ city.

GRAMMAR FOR WRITING (10 marks)

THERE IS / THERE ARE

4 Put the words in order to make sentences.

1 is / city / a / There / big / in / factory / my /_____ .

2 different kinds / There / 700 / over / of British cheese / are / _____ .

3 Paris / many / There / in / museums / are /_____ .

4 large / is / Lahore / There / in / a / mosque /_____ .

5 Papua New Guinea / over / There / in / are / 850 languages /_____ .

ARTICLES

5 Correct the mistakes.

1 The Lake Como is in Italy.

2 He comes from the Morocco.

3 Lots of people live in the New York.

4 There are many modern buildings in United Arab Emirates.

5 Cambodia is in the Asia.

ACADEMIC WRITING SKILLS (15 marks)

6 Write the nationalities.

country	nationality
China	1
Egypt	2
France	3
India	4
Japan	5
Saudi Arabia	6

Thailand	7
The United Arab Emirates	8
The United Kingdom	9
Turkey	10

7 Correct the spelling and punctuation.

1 there are three main islands in new zealand _____

2 the climate is good in malta _____

3 seafood is very popular in greece _____

4 he comes from northern ireland _____

5 there are a lot of interesting museums in berlin _____

TOTAL _____/ 50

REVIEW TEST 5

Name: .... **Date:** ....

READING (10 marks)

Twenty20 cricket: short, fast and exciting!

Cricket is very popular in Australia, New Zealand, England, India, the West Indies and South Africa. Adults and children play cricket. They play in their free time. They usually play on a pitch, but sometimes they play cricket on the beach or in the park.

Twenty20 is a short form of cricket. A match can last two or three hours. It is much quicker than traditional cricket. A traditional one-day cricket match can last seven to eight hours and a test match lasts up to five days.

In Twenty20 cricket, there are two teams of 11 players. One team tries to score points by hitting a ball and the other team tries to stop them. Each team has a limited time – between 75 and 90 minutes. After a short break, the teams change places and the other team tries to score more points to win the game.

Twenty20 cricket is very popular. Large crowds come to watch. Teams must score quickly, so it is fast and exciting. In 2013, Chris Gayle scored 100 runs from 30 balls, a new record for professional cricket.

The Indian Premier League (IPL) is the richest Twenty20 competition. The television rights cost US $1.6 billion. A lot of players from other countries play in the IPL. In 2010, the IPL became the first sport to be shown live on YouTube.

1 Read the text. Write true (T) or false (F) next to the statements.

1 Cricket is very popular in France. ＿＿＿
2 People play cricket on the beach. ＿＿＿
3 Twenty20 is a kind of cricket. ＿＿＿
4 A game of Twenty20 can take five days. ＿＿＿
5 There are 12 players on each team. ＿＿＿
6 Twenty20 cricket is a fast game. ＿＿＿
7 Not many people like to watch Twenty20 cricket. ＿＿＿
8 Chris Gayle is an excellent player. ＿＿＿
9 Players from different countries play in the Indian Premier League. ＿＿＿
10 You cannot watch Twenty20 cricket on the Internet. ＿＿＿

VOCABULARY (10 marks)

2 Write the words from the box in the gaps. You do not need every word.

| national   local   exciting   boring   dangerous   safe   player   fan   million   everywhere   everybody   ticket |

1 A ＿＿＿＿＿＿＿＿＿＿＿ has six '0's – 1,000,000.
2 My favourite football ＿＿＿＿＿＿＿＿＿＿＿ is Cristiano Ronaldo.
3 I buy milk and newspapers from my ＿＿＿＿＿＿＿＿＿＿＿ shop.
4 You can buy a cup of coffee ＿＿＿＿＿＿＿＿＿＿＿ in Rome.
5 Cricket is a slow game. I think it's ＿＿＿＿＿＿＿＿＿＿＿ .
6 The UK has more than ten ＿＿＿＿＿＿＿＿＿＿＿ newspapers.
7 Ice hockey is a ＿＿＿＿＿＿＿＿＿＿＿ sport. Many players are hurt.
8 Toni has a ＿＿＿＿＿＿＿＿＿＿＿ for the concert.

9   Flying is a _____ form of travel.

10 Claire loves athletics. She's a big _____ of Jessica Ennis-Hill.

LANGUAGE DEVELOPMENT (20 marks)

SPORTS COLLOCATIONS

3 Write *play*, *do* or *go* in the gaps.

1 _____ horse-riding   6 _____ rugby

2 _____ swimming   7 _____ squash

3 _____ baseball   8 _____ jogging

4 _____ exercise   9 _____ basketball

5 _____ cricket   10 _____ karate

PREPOSITIONS

4 Write *in* or *on* in the gaps.

1 Ice hockey is a popular sport _____ Canada and North America.

2 You play cricket _____ a pitch.

3 Fans can watch matches _____ a stadium.

4 Thousands of fans watch the matches _____ television.

5 Children play hockey _____ the street in summer.

ADJECTIVES

5 Match the opposites.

cheap	soft
easy	safe
dangerous	exciting
hard	expensive
boring	difficult

GRAMMAR FOR WRITING (10 marks)

SUBJECT – VERB – ADJECTIVE

6 Put the words in order to make sentences.

1 is / dangerous / Karate / .

_____

2 popular / is / Russia / Basketball / in / .

_____

3 Korea / in / a / football player / is / Ki Sung-Yueng / famous / .

_____

4 not / popular / is / Cricket / Albania / in / .

_____

5 for / Tickets / expensive / final / are / the / .

_____

SUBJECT – VERB – ADVERB

7 Correct the sentences.

1 People go horse riding on the park.

_____

2 Swimming lessons are in Thursday evenings.

_____

3 We play cricket in the beach.

_____

4 On summer, we play tennis.

_____

5 I go jogging in Tuesdays.

_____

TOTAL _____ / 50

Name: ....   Date: ....

READING (10 marks)

> **Is your job boring? Here are some different jobs you might like:**
>
> **Zookeeper**
> A zookeeper must like animals. The work is hard and you have to get up early and work long hours. You have to wear a uniform but you don't have to keep it clean. Feeding and cleaning animals can be messy work!
>
> **Astronaut**
> An astronaut must be fit and healthy. Astronauts have to know about a lot of things. They have to know about science and how to fly spacecraft. They also have to train for many years. Astronauts don't have to be men. There are now many women astronauts, too.
>
> **Window cleaner**
> Window cleaners must be fit. They also have to have strong arms. Cleaning tall buildings is dangerous. Window cleaners have to wear safety equipment. They must like heights.
>
> **Pet detective**
> Pet detectives help people find their missing animals. Pet detectives must be friendly because they speak to a lot of people. They also have to use computers. Finding missing pets is difficult. Pet detectives have to be patient. They don't usually have to wear a uniform.

1 Read the text. Write true (T) or false (F) next to the statements.

  1 Zookeepers don't have to wear a uniform. ＿＿＿

  2 Astronauts have to know how to fly spacecraft. ＿＿＿

  3 Astronauts must be men. ＿＿＿

  4 Window cleaners have to clean tall buildings. ＿＿＿

  5 Pet detectives have to wear a uniform. ＿＿＿

2 Read the text again. Write (Z) for *zookeeper*, (A) for *astronaut*, (W) for *window cleaner* or (P) for *pet detective* next to each statement.

  1 He/She must work long hours. ＿＿＿＿＿

  2 He/She has to train for a long time. ＿＿＿＿＿

  3 He/She has to get up early. ＿＿＿＿＿

  4 He/She must be good with people. ＿＿＿＿＿

  5 He/She must be fit and strong. ＿＿＿＿＿

VOCABULARY (10 marks)

3 Write the words from the box in the gaps. You do not need every word.

soon	fitness instructor	great	apply	long hours	gym	link	full-time	fit	part-time	healthy	friendly	fluent

  1 Eating too much fried food is not ＿＿＿＿＿＿＿＿＿＿＿＿＿ .

  2 Toby can run 5 km in 15 minutes. He is very ＿＿＿＿＿＿＿＿＿＿＿＿＿ .

  3 Raza speaks ＿＿＿＿＿＿＿＿＿＿＿＿＿ Urdu and English.

  4 I work ＿＿＿＿＿＿＿＿＿＿＿＿＿ in a restaurant. I only work at the weekends.

5 The students in my new class are very kind and _____ .

6 Anna has a _____ job in a bank. She works from 9 am to 5 pm, Monday to Friday.

7 Open the email and click on the _____ . It will take you to the webpage.

8 We will start the meeting _____ . We are just waiting for Caroline.

9 Kelly works in a sports centre. She's a _____ .

10 Chefs are the first to arrive in the kitchen and the last to leave. They work very _____ .

LANGUAGE DEVELOPMENT (20 marks)

VOCABULARY FOR JOBS

4 Join the phrases to make sentences.

An accountant	looks after animals	in hospital.
A window cleaner	flies spacecraft	in towns and cities.
A builder	gives people medicine	in space.
A chef	looks after passengers	in farms and zoos.
A doctor	looks after money	to different countries.
A pilot	prepares food	in a company.
A fireman	builds houses	in a restaurant.
A flight attendant	puts out fires	on buildings.
An astronaut	cleans windows	on a plane.
A vet	flies planes	in towns and cities.

1 An accountant _____

2 A window cleaner _____

3 A builder _____

4 A chef _____

5 A doctor _____

6 A pilot _____

7 A fireman _____

8 A flight attendant _____

9 An astronaut _____

10 A vet _____

ADJECTIVE PHRASES

5 Circle the best words and phrases.

1 A nurse has to be *good with food / kind and patient*.

2 A pilot doesn't have to be *beautiful / fit and healthy*.

3 A dentist has to be *good with food / smart*.

4 A film director must be *creative / kind and patient*.

5 A fitness instructor doesn't have to be *good with computers / good with people*.

6 A manager has to be *good with people / polite and friendly*.

7 An artist has to be *polite and friendly / creative*.

8 An engineer must be very *intelligent / fit and strong*.
9 A builder has to be *smart / fit and strong*.
10 An accountant doesn't have to be *good with people / intelligent*.

GRAMMAR FOR WRITING (5 marks)

MUST AND HAVE TO

6 Put the words in order to make sentences.

1 does / have / strong / A / be / not / to / dentist / .

_____

2 food / A / good / be / chef / has / with / to / .

_____

3 be / good / have / people / with / to / Nurses / .

_____

4 be / have / creative / Actors / to / .

_____

5 good / does / computers / builder / have / A / to / be / with / not / .

_____

ACADEMIC WRITING SKILLS (5 marks)

CONTRACTIONS

7 Rewrite the sentences without contractions.

1 I'm very tired.

_____

2 I hope you're better.

_____

3 Simone's a good friend.

_____

4 Julia's a clever student.

_____

5 Jack doesn't have to work on Monday.

_____

TOTAL _____ / 50

REVIEW TEST 7

Name: .... **Date:** ....

READING (10 marks)

Aït Benhaddou

What is Aït Benhaddou?
Aït Benhaddou is a fortified village in Morocco. It is in the High Atlas Mountains next to the Ounila River. There is a high wall around the village and there are towers at the corners of the wall. Inside the wall, there are many buildings close together. The wall and the buildings are made from earth. People have to repair the earth buildings regularly because rain damages them.

Who built Aït Benhaddou?
The Berber tribes of North Africa built Aït Benhaddou. They built many towns and villages in the Atlas Mountains. There are over 1,000 villages in the area. Some families still live in the old village of Aït Benhaddou. Most people now live in a newer village on the other side of the river.

Why is Aït Benhaddou famous?
Aït Benhaddou is a very good example of southern Moroccan architecture. Most of the buildings inside the wall are houses. Some are simple but some look like small castles. There is also a mosque, a public square and a caravanserai. Aït Benhaddou is on the old trade route from Sudan to Marrakesh. Groups of travellers stayed in the caravanserai. Aït Benhaddou became a UNESCO World Heritage Site in 1987. The village appears in many films. Scenes from *The Mummy* (1999), *Gladiator* (2000) and *Prince of Persia* (2010) are set here. Many tourists come to visit Aït Benhaddou.

---

1 Read the text. Write true (T) or false (F) next to the statements.

1 Aït Benhaddou is next to the Ounila River in the High Atlas Mountains. ____

2 There are towers and a wall around Aït Benhaddou. ____

3 The houses in Aït Benhaddou are made from wood. ____

4 The Berber people built Aït Benhaddou. ____

5 There are many Berber villages in the mountains. ____

6 Today, the houses of Aït Benhaddou are empty. ____

7 The houses are very strong. ____

8 The houses are very unusual in this part of Morocco. ____

9 Aït Benhaddou is a popular place for film companies. ____

10 Many people visit Aït Benhaddou. ____

LANGUAGE DEVELOPMENT (20 marks)

VOCABULARY FOR BUILDINGS

2 Write the words from the box in the gaps. You do not need every word.

| cinema   ice rink   Library   Museum   Hotel   disco   school   shopping mall |
| Stadium   train station   swimming pool   hospital   supermarket   sports club |

1 There are 147 luxury guest rooms at the _____ de Crillon in Paris.

2 You can watch new films at the _____ .

3 My sister is a doctor at the new _____ .

4 You usually play ice hockey at an _____ .

5 There are over 252 shops in the Westfield _____ in London.

6 85,454 people can watch Real Madrid play football in Santiago Bernabéu _____ .

7 There are over 14 million books in the British _____ in London.

8 Grand Central Terminal in New York is the largest _____ in the world, with 44 platforms.

9 The State Hermitage _____ in Saint Petersburg has over 3 million pieces of art.

10 Crystal Lagoon at San Alfonso del Mar resort, Chile, is 1 km long and up to 35 m deep. It is the largest _____ in the world.

VOCABULARY FOR PARTS OF BUILDINGS

3 Read the text and write the words from the box in the gaps.

| escalator   car park   garden   entrance   exit |

When you arrive at the hotel, you can leave your car in the underground _____ . Enter the building through the _____ and ride on the _____ to the top floor. On the top floor, you can go up the stairs to a café in the roof _____ . If there's a fire or another emergency, leave the building by the nearest _____ .

ADJECTIVES

4 Match the opposites.

ugly	big
cheap	wide
narrow	beautiful
small	old
new	expensive

GRAMMAR FOR WRITING (15 marks)

COMPARATIVE ADJECTIVES

5 Correct the mistakes.

1 The Metropolitan Museum of Art is more popular the Museum of Modern Art.

_____

2 The Chadstone Shopping Centre in Melbourne is more of modern the Westfield Bondi Junction in Sydney.

_____

3 The Shard is more small the Burj Khalifa.

_____

4 Skyscrapers uglyer that old buildings.

_____

5 Taipei 101 taller the Empire State Building.

_____

6 Gold is more expensive that paper.

_____

7 This street is many narrow than the main road.

_____

8 Tokyo is more busy than Vancouver.

_____

9 The island of Sri Lanka is big the island of Sicily.

_____

10 The old market is beautifuller the new shopping mall.

_____

COMPARING QUALITIES

6 Join each pair of sentences to make one sentence with *but*.

1 The Savoy Hotel has more restaurants and bars than the Hotel de Crillon. The Hotel de Crillon is older than the Savoy Hotel.

_____

_____

2 Shinjuku train station is busier than Grand Central Terminal. Grand Central Terminal has more platforms than Shinjuku train station.

_____

_____

3 The Al Wahda shopping mall is bigger than the Westfield shopping mall. The Westfield shopping mall is newer than the Al Wahda shopping mall.

_____

_____

4 The Crystal Lagoon is longer than the Marina Sands Skypark swimming pool.
The Marina Sands Skypark swimming pool is higher than the Crystal Lagoon.

_____

_____

5 The BFI IMAX cinema has a bigger screen than Cinesphere.
Cinesphere can seat more people than the BFI IMAX cinema.

_____

_____

ACADEMIC WRITING SKILLS (5 marks)

SPELLING: DOUBLE CONSONANTS

7 Find the incorrect spellings and correct them.

1 Lucy goes shoping at the weekend. _____

2 Pedro likes going to the sinema. _____

3 Dev has swiming lessons on Thursday afternoons. _____

4 Simon eats in a restorant every Friday. _____

5 Paul goes runing every morning. _____

TOTAL _____ / 50

REVIEW TEST 8

READING (10 marks)

> **Coffee**
>
> Millions of people start their day with a cup of coffee. It is popular all over the world. Coffee has a special smell and flavour. But what is coffee and where does it come from? And how long has it been popular?
>
> Coffee is made from the roasted seeds of the *Coffea arabica* plant. Farmers grow this plant in over 70 countries in South America, Southeast Asia, India and Africa. Coffee is very important for these countries to grow and sell.
>
> Some people say the history of coffee begins in Africa. They say people in Ethiopia were the first to drink coffee. Others say coffee farming began in southern Arabia. We know people drank coffee in fifteenth-century Yemen. From here, coffee spread through the Arab World and on to Turkey. In Turkey, coffee is called *kahve*. This word comes from the Arabic word *qahwah*. From Turkey, coffee went on to Italy and through Europe to Britain. The English word *coffee* comes from the Italian *caffè*.
>
> Coffee is served in many different ways. Some people add milk or cream. This is called white coffee. Other people prefer coffee without milk or cream. This is called black coffee. Some people add sugar or sweetener. You can also drink coffee cold. This is iced coffee. Many people drink coffee for breakfast in the morning. Others enjoy a coffee break at work in the middle of the morning. People also drink coffee after a meal, especially in restaurants.

1 Read the text. Write true (T) or false (F) next to the statements.

   1 Coffee is made from the roasted eggs of *Coffea Arabica*, a small, forest animal. ____

   2 Farmers in South America, Southeast Asia, India and Africa grow coffee. ____

   3 The early history of coffee started in Europe. ____

   4 The Turkish word *kahve* comes from the English word *coffee*. ____

   5 Black coffee hasn't got milk in it. ____

2 Read the text again and answer the questions.

   1 How many countries grow coffee? _____

   2 Where did coffee drinking start? _____

   3 How did coffee spread from Yemen to Britain? _____

   4 What is white coffee? _____

   5 When do people drink coffee? _____

LANGUAGE DEVELOPMENT (20 marks)

VOCABULARY FOR FOOD AND DRINK

3 Read the definitions. Write the words from the box next to the correct definitions. You do not need every word.

> potatoes   dates   milk   honey   onion   chillies   spices   butter   almonds   yoghurt   water   coconut

   1 These are round vegetables. They grow underground. Chips, French fries and crisps are made from them. _____

   2 This is a white liquid. It comes from cows. _____

   3 This is sweet and yellow. Bees make it. _____

4 This is a large fruit. It's brown and hairy on the outside, white on the inside and contains a clear liquid called milk. _____

5 This is a thick white liquid. It's made from milk and sometimes people put fruit or honey in it. _____

6 This is a vegetable with a strong smell and flavour. It's round and has a brown or red skin. It's white inside. _____

7 These are made from plants. People use them in cooking to give special flavour to food. Cinnamon, ginger and cloves are all examples. _____

8 This is a clear liquid, without colour or taste. It is necessary for plant and animal life. It falls from the sky as rain. _____

9 These are small nuts with hard shells. _____

10 These are a sweet fruit. They grow on palm trees. _____

COUNTABLE AND UNCOUNTABLE NOUNS

4 Write the words from the box in the correct columns.

potatoes dates milk honey onion spices butter yoghurt water chillies

countable nouns	uncountable nouns

GRAMMAR FOR WRITING (15 marks)

SUBJECT–VERB AGREEMENT

5 Correct the mistakes.

1 Arab restaurants serves *sharwarma* and *kabsa*.

_____

2 Cambodian cuisine use a lot of fruit.

_____

3 Seafood are popular in many restaurants in Greece.

_____

4 A famous dish from Korea are *kim chee*.

_____

5 Two popular dishes in Turkey is called *dolma* and *gözleme*.

_____

6 Thai food are served with rice and vegetables.

_____

7 Moroccan chefs prepares *tajine* dishes.

_____

8 Kebabs is served in pita bread.

_____

9 Indian chefs makes curries with vegetables and spices.

   _____

10 Rice are popular in Japan.

   _____

DETERMINERS: A, AN AND SOME

6 Correct the mistakes.

1 Some popular rice dish in Spain is *paella*.

   _____

2 There are some potato in *Lancashire hotpot*.

   _____

3 Italian like eating pizza and pasta.

   _____

4 Ethiopian chefs prepares *tibs* with meat and some vegetables.

   _____

5 Turkish cooks add a egg to *menemen*.

   _____

ACADEMIC WRITING SKILLS (5 marks)

SPELLING

7 Rearrange the letters to spell adjectives for food and drink.

1 tewes _____

2 yavuros _____

3 usocelidi _____

4 cyips _____

5 yehatlh _____

TOTAL _____ / 50

Name: .... **Date:** ....

READING (10 marks)

Animals of India

India has some of the most beautiful animals in the world. They live in the mountains, the desert and the forests. Over 250 types of animal in India are in danger. The Indian government protects these animals. There are over 500 wildlife sanctuaries. These are safe places for animals to live.

Indian Elephant
The Indian elephant (*Elephas maximus indicus*) is smaller than the African elephant. They also have smaller ears. Females are usually smaller than males. Indian elephants reach a height of between 2 and 3.5 m at their shoulders. They can weigh between 2,000 and 5,000 kg. They eat about 150 kg of plants every day. Elephants live to between 50 and 70 years old.

Royal Bengal Tiger
Tigers (*Panthera tigris*) are famous around the world. They are the largest type of cat. They live in national parks all over India. Males grow between 275 and 290 cm long. They weigh between 135 and 230 kg. They have a lifespan of 10–15 years in the wild. Every tiger has stripes but they all have different patterns. A tiger can eat up to 40 kg of meat at one time. Tigers in zoos eat 5–6 kg a day. There are now only 2,000 tigers in India.

Lion-tailed Macaque
Many types of monkey live in India. Lion-tailed macaques (*Macaca silenus*) are found in southwest India. Their bodies are black. The hair around their faces is grey. Their bodies are between 40 and 60 cm and their tails are about 25 cm. They weigh 3 to 10 kg. They can live for more than 30 years in zoos but their lifespan is shorter in the wild. They live in mountain forests in southwest India. They eat leaves, fruit and nuts. Lion-tailed macaques only live in India.

---

1 Read the text and answer the questions.

  1 What is a wildlife sanctuary?_____

  2 What are the differences between an Indian elephant and an African elephant?_____

  3 Where do tigers live in India today?_____

  4 How many tigers are there in India?_____

  5 Where do lion-tailed macaques live?_____

2 Complete the table with information from the text.

scientific name	Elephas maximus indicus	Panthera tigris	Macaca silenus
common name			
size (cm)			
weight (kg)			
lifespan (years)			
food			

VOCABULARY (5 marks)

3 Decide if the bold words are nouns or verbs. Write *noun* or *verb* after each one.

1 The average healthy tiger can **run** at about 56 kph.

_____

2 Young wolves, lions and bears are called **cubs**.

_____

3 Eagles can **catch** fish in rivers and lakes.

_____

4 Leopards **hunt** many animals, from gazelles to monkeys.

_____

5 Jaguars look for their **prey** in jungles.

_____

LANGUAGE DEVELOPMENT (15 marks)

CAN AND CANNOT

4 Correct the mistakes.

1 Lions can survives without water for four or five days.
2 Lions can to communicate with other lions by roaring.
3 You can hearing a lion roar from 8 km away.
4 A male lion cans weigh 250 kg.
5 Lions no can run for long distances.

DESCRIBING FACTS ABOUT ANIMALS

5 Write the words from the box in the gaps.

at (x2)   for   on   in

1 Pandas live _____ China.
2 Cheetahs can run _____ about 115 kph.
3 Crocodiles can live _____ 60–70 years.
4 Vultures can fly _____ more than 35 kph.
5 Bees live _____ nectar and pollen.

VOCABULARY FOR ANIMALS

6 Write the words from the box in the gaps.

| endangered   harmless   nocturnal   amphibious   venomous |

1 A snakebite can be dangerous – some snakes are _____ .
2 Crocodiles are _____. They can live on land and in water.
3 Mountain gorillas are _____. There are very few of them in the wild.
4 People do not like spiders but most of them are _____ to humans.
5 Owls are _____ birds. They hunt at night.

GRAMMAR FOR WRITING (5 marks)

SUPERLATIVE ADJECTIVES

7 Put the words and phrases in order to make sentences.

1 in the world / fastest / The / is / cheetah / the / animal / .

_____

2 most / sea / the / is / snake / venomous / The / snake / .

_____

3 Ulysses / most / butterfly / of / is / in the world / one / The / the / butterflies / beautiful / .

_____

4 Tiger / of / deadliest / sharks / one / are / the / in the world / fish / .

_____

5 in the world / The / whale / biggest / is / the / shark / fish / .

_____

ACADEMIC WRITING SKILLS (15 marks)

SPELLING

8 Read the definitions and write the missing letters to complete the animal words.

1 b _ _ _   A large, strong animal with the Latin name Ursus.
2 b _ _ _   An animal which has wings and feathers.
3 b _ _   An animal like a mouse with wings which flies at night.
4 w _ _ _   A wild animal of the dog family.
5 i _ _ _ _ _   A small animal with six legs.
6 f _ _ _ _ _   A fast bird which can be trained to hunt other birds.
7 b _ _   A yellow and black insect which makes honey.
8 s _ _ _ _ _   A small animal with eight legs which catches insects in a web.
9 s _ _ _ _   A large fish with sharp teeth.
10 l _ _ _   A large animal of the cat family which lives in Africa.

PUNCTUATION

9 Add capital letters and punctuation to the sentences.

1 many dangerous animals live in south america

_____

2 one of the most dangerous fish in south america is the piranha

_____

3 piranhas live in south american rivers like the amazon and the orinoco

_____

4 they normally grow between 14 and 26 cm long

_____

5 piranhas eat insects fish and small animals

_____

TOTAL _____/ 50

REVIEW TEST 10

Name: .... Date: ....

READING (5 marks)

Space tourism

Do you like adventure? Are you looking for a holiday with a difference? Are you tired of beach holidays? Why not try a different kind of holiday?

Space tourism means going on holiday in a spacecraft. It's expensive at the moment, but more and more people are hoping to enjoy space travel in the future. Space tourism started in 2001 with visits to the International Space Station (ISS). Tourists went there in the Soyuz spacecraft. The flights were very expensive. They cost between US$ 20 and 35 million.

The first space tourist was Dennis Tito, an American businessman. He studied Engineering and he is interested in space. He spent seven days on the ISS and he did scientific experiments. Russia stopped its space tourism programme in 2010 because more scientists wanted to go to the space station. They plan to offer tourist flights in the future.

Several companies plan to offer flights into space for much less money in the future. Tourists will experience zero gravity and float around the spacecraft. The views of Earth from a spacecraft in orbit are amazing.

1 Read the text. Write true (T) or false (F) next to the statements below.

1 Space tourism is expensive at the moment. ____
2 The first space tourists went to the International Space Station in 2010. ____
3 Dennis Tito is a Russian businessman. ____
4 Dennis Tito spent a week on the International Space Station. ____
5 Space tourism will become more expensive in the future. ____

LANGUAGE DEVELOPMENT (20 marks)

QUANTIFIERS

2 Write quantifiers from the box in the gaps. More than one answer is possible.

| many   most   a lot of   not many   a few   some |

1 _____ (83%) people in Florida drive to work.
2 _____ (4%) people in Florida walk to work.
3 _____ (2%) people in Florida take public transport to work.
4 _____ (1.5%) people in Florida ride a bike to work.
5 _____ (3%) people in California ride a bike to work.
6 _____ (74%) people in California drive to work.
7 _____ (5%) people in California take public transport to work.
8 _____ (27%) people in New York take public transport to work.
9 _____ (7%) people in New York walk to work.
10 _____ (4%) people in Texas walk to work.

TRANSPORT COLLOCATIONS

3 Write *by*, *to* or *from* in the gaps.

1 Most students take the bus _____ university.

2 My brother goes to work _____ train.

3 Commuters travel to and _____ work every day.

4 My grandmother takes a taxi _____ the shopping centre.

5 Many people get to work _____ motorbike.

4 Write the verbs from the box in the gaps.

ride   rides (x2)   drives   takes

1 Luke _____ a motorbike to college.

2 Carlos _____ his car to work.

3 Lucy _____ a horse after school on Thursdays.

4 Gerald usually _____ a bus to the airport.

5 In Amsterdam, 40% of people _____ their bike every day.

GRAMMAR FOR WRITING (15 marks)

SUBJECT – VERB – OBJECT

5 Correct the mistakes.

1 Commuters in Paris take the metro work.

_____

2 Some commuters in Japan travel plane.

_____

3 Many commuters in Istanbul go the ferry to work.

_____

4 In Saigon, families often travel a motorbike to work and school.

_____

5 Some students in California drives to university.

_____

6 A few students takes the bus.

_____

7 Most students to college a bike ride.

_____

8 Not many people in Dhaka travel to work by a taxi.

_____

9 Many commuters in Sydney drive the train to work.

_____

10 In Dubai, commuters by car travel to work.

_____

LINKING SENTENCES WITH PRONOUNS

6 Match sentences 1–5 with sentences a–e. Use the bold words to help you.

1 Jane goes to work on foot.

2 Sarah and Vanessa drive to university.

3 Sander cycles to work in Amsterdam.

4 Many commuters in New York take the ferry.

5 People in London take **the Underground**.

a They go across the river.

b It is faster than the bus.

c She gets fit walking.

d He rides on special roads for bicycles.

e They live a long way away.

ACADEMIC WRITING SKILLS (10 marks)

ERROR CORRECTION

7 Look at a student's paragraph marked with correction codes. Correct the mistakes.

Correction codes		
[G] = grammar	[MW] = missing word	[P] = punctuation
[C] = content (is the information correct?)		[WP] = wrong preposition.

Popular means of transport for commuters in the USA

The table show [G] how americans [P] commute to work. There are five types of transport: driving a car alone, sharing a car, taking public transport, cycling and walking. In 43 states, more [MW] 75% of children [C] drive a car alone [MW] work. In new york [P], 50% of commuter [G] use other ways to get by [WP] work. About 14% of commuters share a car to work in Alaska and Hawaii, the highest percentage in the UK. [C] Most people in New York use public transport. Here, 28% take a train, subway or bus. In Alabama, Arkansas, Maine and Mississippi, 1% of commuters use public transport. Bicycling and walking are not popular forms of public transport at [WP] the USA.

TOTAL _____ / 50

WRITING TASK 1 MODEL ANSWER

Write about somebody in your family.

My uncle's name is Ahmad Al Ali. He is 37. My uncle is a doctor. He works in a hospital. Ahmad lives with his family.
He and his wife live in Doha in Qatar. My uncle speaks Arabic, English and a little bit of Urdu. He has one daughter and one son. They are very small.

ADDITIONAL WRITING TASK

Complete this personal profile with information about yourself and write a paragraph for the My Life section. Look at Amir Khan's personal profile on Student's Book page 19 for ideas.

FriendNet

My profile: _____

My personal information
First name: _____
Last name: _____
Date of birth: _____
City: _____
Country: _____
Languages: _____
Job: _____

My address
Email: _____

My family
Mother: _____
Father: _____
Brother(s): _____
Sister(s): _____

My hobbies and interests
Hobbies: _____
Favourite football club: _____
Favourite sportsman/sportswoman: _____

Write facts about the weather in your city.

Palawan is in the Philippines. Palawan has two seasons. The seasons are the dry season and the wet season. The dry season is from December to May. It is dry and windy. The average temperatures are from 21 °C to 29 °C. The average rainfall is from 10 mm to 176 mm. The rainy season is from June to November. It is wet and warm. The average temperatures are from 24 °C to 31 °C. The average rainfall is from 199 mm to 439 mm.

ADDITIONAL WRITING TASK

Research the weather in a country you would like to visit on holiday. Find out about the climate and the best time to visit. Complete the text below.

_____ (country) **weather**

Home| Weather|Climate | Weather Averages |

_____ (country) is in _____ (the south/north/east/west). The climate in _____ (country)
is _____ _____ It has _____ seasons:

- _____ _____.
  Each season lasts for _____ months.
- the _____ season and the _____ season.
  _____ lasts for _____ months _____ lasts for _____months.

(Describe a season. Which months does the season start and finish? What are the average temperatures?
What is the average rainfall? What is the weather like?)

_____
_____
_____
_____
_____
_____

WRITING TASK 3 MODEL ANSWER

Write facts about the lifestyle of a student in your class.

Adel is a student in my class. This is his timetable. Adel studies English and Management. He gets up at 7 am. On Monday, Tuesday and Thursday, he has English classes from 9 to 12. He has lunch at 12.15 every day. He has Maths at 2 pm on Tuesday and Wednesday. Every day, he studies in the library from 3 pm to 5 pm. In the evenings, he plays football or video games. On Saturday, he goes to the cinema.

ADDITIONAL WRITING TASK

Write about typical lifestyles in your country. Look at the text about the lifestyle of the Kombai people on Student's Book page 55. Describe the typical lifestyles of people in your country so that a Kombai person could read and find out about your country.

Life in _____ is very _____ .

People usually get up every morning at _____ . They go to bed at
_____ .

(Write what people typically do in your country.)

Men _____
_____ .

Women _____
_____ .

Children
_____ .
_____ .

(Write what people typically eat, where they live and the things they have.)

_____
_____
_____

Parents teach their children _____
_____

The most important part of life in my country is _____
_____

WRITING TASK 4 MODEL ANSWER

Write facts about your country.

The Republic of the Seychelles is in the Indian Ocean. There are 115 islands in the Seychelles. The population of the Seychelles is 86,000 people. The capital city is Victoria. The climate in the Seychelles is warm and humid. People in the Seychelles speak Creole, French and English. Many children learn English at school. Most people in the Seychelles are Christian. There are also some Muslim and Hindu people. The currency of the Seychelles is the rupee. Tourism and fishing are the most important industries in the Seychelles. Most people work in tourism. The Seychelles are famous for their fish and seafood.

ADDITIONAL WRITING TASK

Choose a country to write about. Look at the topics in the wordbox and put them in a logical order in the table. You can add more topics of your own to the list. Research the country using the Internet and add key words for each topic to the table. Use the completed table to help you write sentences about the country.

| language currency population food |
| capital city industry climate geography |

	topic	key words for topic
1		
2		
3		
4		
5		
6		
7		
8		

WRITING TASK 5 MODEL ANSWER

Write facts about a popular sport in your country.

Cricket is very popular in Sri Lanka. Young people and old people like to play cricket. Sri Lankan people play cricket in the parks and in the stadiums. In Sri Lanka, people play cricket in the summer and in the winter. Muttiah Muralitharan is a famous cricket player from Sri Lanka. Over 2 billion people watch cricket. You can watch cricket at the R. Premadasa Stadium in Colombo. The tickets are expensive.

ADDITIONAL WRITING TASK

1 Choose a country. Research two sports that are popular in that country. Make an ideas map below for the two sports. Include information on:
   • the people who like the sport (*age, male/female, number*)
   • the type of sport (*ball game/team game/martial art*)
   • the places people play/do the sport
   • the times of day/year or seasons people play/do the sport
   • the names of famous sportsmen or women in the sport
   • how many people/fans watch the sport
   • where you can see the sport
   • the price of tickets.
2 Use your ideas map to write about the sports.

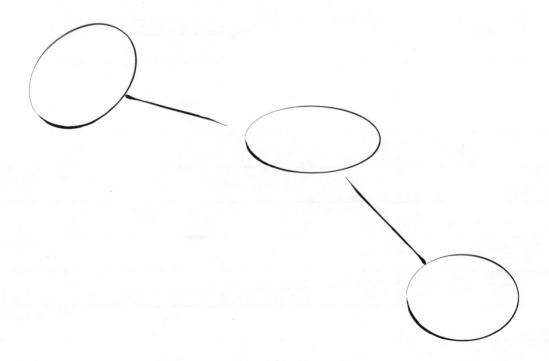

WRITING TASK 6 MODEL ANSWER

Write a description of a job for a friend.

Dear Iman,

I hope you're well. I have a great job for you. I think you'll like it – it's in Japan.

The job is in Sapporo. It's a big city in the north. The job is for a manager. It's full-time. The salary is 400,000 yen a month. You must have a university degree in business and administration. You have to speak English. You don't have to speak Japanese. You must be good with people and you have to work long hours. You also have to be very good with computers.

Here's the link: www.discoverjobs4you.com

Good luck!

Mariam

ADDITIONAL WRITING TASK

Choose one of the jobs below and write an email to a friend telling them about it.

a

◀▶ C ⌂	www.find_my_job.com	⊖ ⊜ ⊗

FIND A JOB   GET HELP!   UPLOAD YOUR CV

Your search

Area(s): <u>Business</u>

Job(s): <u>Manager</u>

✉ Email me jobs like this

🔊 RSS Feeds

Location

⬇ Shanghai, China

Hanlu Electronics

Hanlu Electronics is a growing company that produces electrical parts for large companies.

We are looking for a business manager to work at the company and help us expand our business.

Required: work long days; travel overseas; have 10 years' experience

Desirable: speak fluent Chinese and English

Salary: CNY 30,000 per month

Type: Full-time (including some weekends)

b

www.find_my_job.com

FIND A **JOB**   GET **HELP!**   UPLOAD YOUR **CV**

Your search

Area(s): Architecture

Job(s): Architect

✉ Email me jobs like this

🔊 RSS Feeds

Location

⬇ India

Mumbai Architecture Solutions

Mumbai Architecture Solutions is a small company in Mumbai.
We design commercial and residential buildings.

We are looking for an architect. All our architects are qualified.

Required: 2 years' experience and work some weekends

Desired: speak English (not essential); work long days

Salary: INR 900,000 per month

Type: Part-time

c

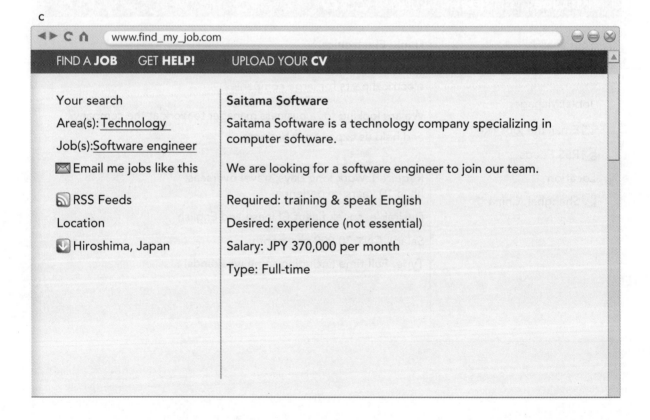

www.find_my_job.com

FIND A **JOB**   GET **HELP!**   UPLOAD YOUR **CV**

Your search

Area(s): Technology

Job(s): Software engineer

✉ Email me jobs like this

🔊 RSS Feeds

Location

⬇ Hiroshima, Japan

Saitama Software

Saitama Software is a technology company specializing in computer software.

We are looking for a software engineer to join our team.

Required: training & speak English

Desired: experience (not essential)

Salary: JPY 370,000 per month

Type: Full-time

WRITING TASK 7 MODEL ANSWER

Write a comparison of two buildings.

The Istanbul Cevahir and the SM Mall of Asia are two modern malls. The Istanbul Cevahir is in Istanbul in Turkey and the SM Mall of Asia is in Manila in the Philippines. The Istanbul Cevahir is older than the SM Mall of Asia, but it is bigger. The Istanbul Cevahir and the SM Mall of Asia have six floors. The SM Mall of Asia has more shops than the Istanbul Cevahir. It also has more restaurants, but the Istanbul Cevahir has more cinemas than the SM Mall of Asia.

ADDITIONAL WRITING TASK

Write a comparison of the Petronas Towers and the Shard, using the information in the table and the questions below. Find pictures of these buildings on the Internet for your answers to questions 9 and 10.

	Petronas Towers	The Shard
country	Malaysia	United Kingdom
city	Kuala Lumpur	London
height (m)	452	309.6
year	1999	2013
number of floors	88	95
number of lifts	78	44
flights of stairs	1,765	306
cost (USD)	850,000,000	660,000,000

1 Write the names of the buildings.
2 Write the location of the buildings.
3 Compare the size of the buildings.
4 Compare the age of the buildings.
5 Compare the number of floors in the buildings.
6 Compare the number of lifts in the buildings.
7 Compare the flights of stairs (= set of stairs from one floor to another) in the buildings.
8 Compare the cost of the buildings.
9 Which building is more creative/interesting/exciting/modern?
10 Which building do you like? Why?

WRITING TASK 8 MODEL ANSWER

Write about food in your country for a student website.

Korean food

At a Korean restaurant, you can find many different kinds of soup, fish, beef and rice dishes. Kimchi and banchan are very popular. Korean food is also famous for noodle dishes. Kimchi is made from vegetables. It is served with soup, rice and meat. It is spicy and healthy. Banchan are small and tasty dishes. They are served with some rice.

ADDITIONAL WRITING TASK

Write about Italian or Indian cuisine for a student website. Research the cuisines using the Internet and find out about two more typical dishes, what they are made with and how they are served. Complete the notes below. Then write texts like the ones on pages 147 and 150 of the Student's Book.

Italian food	Indian food
Popular dishes:	Popular dishes:
1) Spaghetti Bolognese made with: beef, onions, tomatoes and spaghetti served with: cheese and black pepper	1) Chicken Korma made with: chicken, yoghurt, cream, coconut milk, almonds served with: rice and naan bread
2) made with: served with:	2) made with: served with:
3) made with: served with:	3) made with: served with:

WRITING TASK 9 MODEL ANSWER

Write a paragraph about an animal.

Polar bears (*Ursus maritimus*) are the biggest bears. The average polar bear is 250 to 300 cm high and weighs between 350 and 480 kg. Polar bears are not the fastest bears. Brown bears can run faster than polar bears. Polar bears can run at about 35 to 40 kph. Polar bears live for about 23 to 25 years. They live on seals. Polar bears live in the Arctic Circle. There are about 23,000 polar bears in the world today. They are not the most endangered bears. Panda bears are more endangered.

ADDITIONAL WRITING TASK

Write a paragraph about one of the sharks in the table. Compare it with the other sharks in the table using comparative and superlative adjectives.

Three types of shark

scientific name	*Carcharodon carcharias*	*Galeocerdo cuvier*	*Rhincodon typus*
common name	great white shark	tiger shark	whale shark
size (cm)	370–500	325–425	760–1,200
weight (kg)	2,268	385–635	13,600
average speed (kph)	3.2	3.85	5
lifespan (years)	c. 30	c. 20–25	c. 60–100
diet	fish, sea lions and seals	fish, seals and turtles	plankton, krill and small squid
habitat	cool waters	warm and cool waters	warm waters

WRITING TASK 10 MODEL ANSWER

Write a paragraph about transport in your city.

This report shows the results of a survey of transport in Al Ain. Over 568,000 people live in the city. Figure 1 shows average travel times in Al Ain. Figure 2 shows popular means of transport in Al Ain.

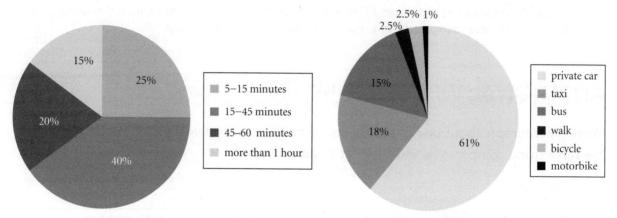

Figure 1: Average travel times in Al Ain

Figure 2: Popular means of transport in Al Ain

There are six forms of transport in Al Ain: cars, taxis, buses, bicycles, motorbikes and walking. The most popular form of transport is the private car. Most people (over 60%) drive their cars to work. Taxis are more popular than buses. 18% of the people in Al Ain use taxis to get to work and 15% of people use buses. Taxis and buses are more popular than cycling and walking. A few people (5%) walk to work or cycle. Only 1% of the people in Al Ain ride a motorbike to work. The traffic in Al Ain is heavy in the morning and in the afternoon. It takes about 30 minutes to get to work or school in the morning.

ADDITIONAL WRITING TASK

The table shows the results of a survey of transport use in London and New York. Write a paragraph describing the information.

London: Average time travelling to work: 37.5 minutes.
New York City: Average time travelling to work: 30.4 minutes

Means of transport	London	New York
Car	11%	30%
Motorbike	2%	2%
Bicycle	3%	1%
Bus	12%	14%
Train	40%	2%
Underground/Subway	28%	41%
On foot	4%	10%

ACKNOWLEDGEMENTS

Thanks to all the team at Cambridge University Press for their help, ideas and advice, particularly Barry Tadman and Frances Disken and Janet Weller for handling the proof stages. Thanks also to my family, Sarah and Stanley, for their support.
Andrew Scott

Publisher acknowledgements

The publishers are extremely grateful to the following people and their students for reviewing and trialling this course during its development. The course has benefited hugely from your insightful comments, advice and feedback.

Mr M.K. Adjibade, King Saud University, Saudi Arabia; Canan Aktug, Bursa Technical University, Turkey; Olwyn Alexander, Heriot Watt University, UK; Valerie Anisy, Damman University, Saudi Arabia; Anwar Al-Fetlawi, University of Sharjah, UAE; Laila Al-Qadhi, Kuwait University, Kuwait; Tahani Al-Taha, University of Dubai, UAE; Ozlem Atalay, Middle East Technical University, Turkey; Seda Merter Ataygul, Bursa Technical University Turkey; Harika Altug, Bogazici University, Turkey; Kwab Asare, University of Westminster, UK; Erdogan Bada, Cukurova University, Turkey; Cem Balcikanli, Gazi University, Turkey; Gaye Bayri, Anadolu University, Turkey; Meher Ben Lakhdar, Sohar University, Oman; Emma Biss, Girne American University, UK; Dogan Bulut, Meliksah University, Turkey; Sinem Bur, TED University, Turkey; Alison Chisholm, University of Sussex, UK; Dr. Panidnad Chulerk , Rangsit University, Thailand; Sedat Cilingir, Bilgi University, Istanbul, Turkey; Sarah Clark, Nottingham Trent International College, UK; Elaine Cockerham, Higher College of Technology, Muscat, Oman; Asli Derin, Bilgi University, Turkey; Steven Douglass, University of Sunderland, UK; Jacqueline Einer, Sabanci University, Turkey; Basak Erel, Anadolu University, Turkey; Hande Lena Erol, Piri Reis Maritime University, Turkey; Gulseren Eyuboglu, Ozyegin University, Turkey; Muge Gencer, Kemerburgaz University, Turkey; Jeff Gibbons, King Fahed University of Petroleum and Minerals, Saudi Arabia; Maxine Gilway, Bristol University, UK; Dr Christina Gitsaki, HCT, Dubai Men's College, UAE; Sam Fenwick, Sohar University, Oman; Peter Frey, International House, Doha, Qatar; Neil Harris, Swansea University, UK; Vicki Hayden, College of the North Atlantic, Qatar; Ajarn Naratip Sharp Jindapitak, Prince of Songkla University, Hatyai, Thailand; Joud Jabri-Pickett, United Arab Emirates University, Al Ain, UAE; Aysel Kilic, Anadolu University, Turkey; Ali Kimav, Anadolu University, Turkey; Bahar Kiziltunali, Izmir University of Economics, Turkey; Kamil Koc, Ozel Kasimoglu Coskun Lisesi, Turkey; Ipek Korman-Tezcan, Yeditepe University, Turkey; Philip Lodge, Dubai Men's College, UAE; Iain Mackie, Al Rowdah University, Abu Dhabi, UAE; Katherine Mansfield, University of Westminster, UK; Kassim Mastan, King Saud University, Saudi Arabia; Elspeth McConnell, Newham College, UK; Lauriel Mehdi, American University of Sharjah, UAE; Dorando Mirkin-Dick, Bell International Institute, UK; Dr Sita Musigrungsi, Prince of Songkla University, Hatyai, Thailand; Mark Neville, Al Hosn University, Abu Dhabi, UAE; Shirley Norton, London School of English, UK; James Openshaw, British Study Centres, UK; Hale Ottolini, Mugla Sitki Kocman University, Turkey; David Palmer, University of Dubai, UAE; Michael Pazinas, United Arab Emirates University, UAE; Troy Priest, Zayed University, UAE; Alison Ramage Patterson, Jeddah, Saudi Arabia; Paul Rogers, Qatar Skills Academy, Qatar; Josh Round, Saint George International, UK; Harika Saglicak,

Bogazici University, Turkey; Asli Saracoglu, Isik University, Turkey; Neil Sarkar, Ealing, Hammersmith and West London College, UK; Nancy Shepherd, Bahrain University, Bahrain; Jonathan Smith, Sabanci University, Turkey; Peter Smith, United Arab Emirates University, UAE; Adem Soruc, Fatih University Istanbul, Turkey; Dr Peter Stanfield, HCT, Madinat Zayed & Ruwais Colleges, UAE; Maria Agata Szczerbik, United Arab Emirates University, Al Ain, UAE; Burcu Tezcan-Unal, Bilgi University, Turkey; Dr Nakonthep Tipayasuparat, Rangsit University, Thailand; Scott Thornbury, The New School, New York, USA; Susan Toth, HCT, Dubai Men's Campus, Dubai, UAE; Melin Unal, Ege University, Izmir, Turkey; Aylin Unaldi, Bogaziçi University, Turkey; Colleen Wackrow, Princess Nourah bint Abdulrahman University, Riyadh, Saudi Arabia; Gordon Watts, Study Group, Brighton UK; Po Leng Wendelkin, INTO at University of East Anglia, UK; Halime Yildiz, Bilkent University, Ankara, Turkey; Ferhat Yilmaz, Kahramanmaras Sutcu Imam University, Turkey.

Special thanks to Peter Lucantoni for sharing his expertise, both pedagogical and cultural.

Special thanks also to Michael Pazinas for writing the Research projects which feature at the end of every unit. Michael has first-hand experience of teaching in and developing materials for the paperless classroom. He has worked in Greece, the Middle East and the UK. Prior to his current position as Curriculum and Assessment Coordinator for the Foundation Program at the United Arab Emirates University he was an English teacher for the British Council, the University of Exeter and several private language institutes. Michael is also a graphic designer, involved in instructional design and educational eBook development.

Photos

p.8: (1) © Eric Limon/Shutterstock; p.8: (2) © szefai/ Shutterstock; p.8: (3) © Steven Vidler/Eurasia Press/Corbis. All other video stills are by kind permission of © Discovery Communication, LLC 2014.

Dictionary

Cambridge dictionaries are the world's most widely used dictionaries for learners of English. Available at three levels (Cambridge Essential English Dictionary, Cambridge Learner's Dictionary and Cambridge Advanced Learner's Dictionary), they provide easy-to-understand definitions, example sentences, and help in avoiding typical mistakes. The dictionaries are also available online at dictionary.cambridge.org. © Cambridge University Press, reproduced with permission.

Corpus

Development of this publication has made use of the Cambridge English Corpus (CEC). The CEC is a multi-billion word computer database of contemporary spoken and written English. It includes British English, American English and other varieties of English. It also includes the Cambridge Learner Corpus, developed in collaboration with Cambridge English Language Assessment. Cambridge University Press has built up the CEC to provide evidence about language use that helps to produce better language teaching materials.

Typeset by Integra.